"Dementia: Pathways to hope ... challenge to all carers, families, and ... 'R ... who have dementia. The Bible teaches, ... spirits are being renewed every day' (2 Corinthians 4:16). Louise gives an example of this in the person of William: 'Simply being in church, with its ritual and hymns he has always loved and its sense of peace was like being at home. It resonates with the life-long practices and beliefs at the core of his being.' Louise has a very gifted, personal style of writing. She does not only write with the mind but also from her heart and wide experience."

Paul and Dr Ruth Bullivant, retired pastor, evangelist and Christian counsellor.

"... e chaplaincy taught me that illness of any kind can concern and engage the whole person, as well as family and carers. Dementia is no exception, and this excellent book is vital for keeping us focused on engaging holistically, not only with the dementia sufferer, but with all their carers and supporters."

– Revd Chris Wood, Director, Bridge Christian Counselling Centre.

"A must read, this treasure trove of information and ideas gives practical and helpful suggestions for communities, churches and carers. 'Doing good' to each other would need to become our way of life, which is what Christ intended. The emphasis is on real practical, spiritual, and emotional help for the 'trapped carer' in the later isolating stages of dementia. Louise's insightful psychological and spiritual applications could improve the mental wellbeing of sufferers and helpers alike."

– Deryn van der Tang was carer for her late husband, who had vascular dementia, and now provides support for elderly Christians at Dorothea Court in Bedford.

"It has been my privilege in nursing and caring for older people for over forty ye ... ee what a difference spiritual encouragement makes to the older Cl ... n. It is their lifeline, something that is absolutely vital to their wellbeing, and even more so in the midst of dementia. How wonderful then, that this book on hope has been written within the context of dementia. Trying to come to terms with a diagnosis of dementia can be heartbreaki... great encouragem... ned by *their circumstances. She reminds the reader of their security in Christ and that no illness can change who they are in Him."*

– **Janet Jacob,** former psychogeriatric nurse and care home manager.

"Louise has given a sensitive and passionate presentation of careful research and case studies, and throughout has pointed out the pathways to hope the title suggests. The scripture gives an edict to operate as a caring and supportive community and never has the need been so great as today when we are surrounded by fragmented families. This is a must read and an inspiration to action for all Christians."

– **Revd Carol Taplin,** Chaplaincy Manager, Aneurin Bevan University Health Board.

"Louise Morse's fourth book gives dementia sufferers, care givers, and professionals in the field much to reflect on. With a background of years within the care provision sector and a Master's Degree in cognitive behavioural therapy (CBT), Louise faces the difficulties of living with dementia as a sufferer or caregiver head on. Neither does she avoid issues raised by the recent 'Dementia Friendly Communities' initiatives from Government and dementia pressure groups. Challenging, even unsettling at times, Dementia: Pathways to Hope *inspires, as Louise draws on her experience and her vibrant, Christian faith to remind us that our God-given personhood remains intact despite illness and that the Holy Spirit still empowers all who seek Him."*

– **Fran Waddams,** Theology Graduate and Religious Studies teacher.

"Dementia is having an impact on people of all ages, not just the elderly. Families, friends, and church fellowships are all being affected. Louise's Pathways to Hope *highlights the importance of guarding the heart, and of being strengthened in our spirits for whatever life brings us, whether or not it includes dementia. This book contains much helpful information and is enlightening and encouraging: it will help individuals and churches alike."*

– **Clyde Thomas,** Senior Pastor, Victory Church, Cwmbran, South Wales.

"Passionate and compassionate, Louise Morse writes with authority about the increasingly feared modern 'plague' we know as dementia. Working with a nationwide organisation – many of whose clients suffer from dementia – she has extensive experience of its different forms. This book does much to remove the sting from those who face the condition in

themselves, their family or their friends. It does contain signposts to that elusive element in dementia – hope. The book is packed with examples, practical advice and accessible medical information. Louise is not afraid to criticise national policies, and commend them occasionally! She challenges and helps churches and church leaders to meet the needs of sufferers and carers. She encourages carers in their often lonely life with practical tips and Biblical wisdom. Dementia is something we will all meet sooner or later. Christians are called to love, and a part of loving is understanding. I learned a lot from this book. I am sure you will too. Do read it."

– Revd Michael Wenham, author of *My Donkeybody*.

"Lou Morse is one of the most popular speakers at our exhibitions when it comes to the subject of how the church needs to tackle the problems of members of the congregation who have issues affecting the brain's capacity. She is known as an expert in this area. This book takes all that knowledge and puts it into language that can be understood by those who are not experts, but are having to learn what to do when you have someone who is suffering and you need to be able to respond. This book has helped my wife and me cope with a friend who now has diminished mental capacity. Highly recommended."

– Bill Allen, Event Director, Christian Resources Exhibition.

"In her book, Dementia: Pathways to Hope, *Louise Morse acknowledges many of the wider issues of our modern living which may be having a negative impact on our health, from globalization, change in communities and fragmentation of family life, and explores whether they may be contributing to people developing dementia. But throughout the book, Louise clearly demonstrates that there is HOPE, both for the person with dementia and their caregiver. Louise lifts you heavenwards and states that Christians are the bearers of the most powerful communicator in this universe – the Holy Spirit, which enables people to connect with those with dementia at an eternal level. This amazing book encompasses the multidimensional aspects of dementia with plenty of practical advice. Louise continually draws you onto the Pathway of Hope, at the level where our solid hope is in God and His promises."*

– Rosie Barker, RN DN, former care home manager

Books by the same author:

Could It Be Dementia? Losing Your Mind Doesn't Mean Losing Your Soul , Monarch Books, 2008

Dementia: Frank and Linda's Story, Monarch Books, 2010

Worshipping with Dementia: Meditations, Scriptures and Prayers for Sufferers and Carers, Monarch Books, 2010

Dementia:
Pathways to Hope

Spiritual insights and practical advice

Louise Morse

MONARCH
BOOKS

Oxford UK, and Grand Rapids, USA

To Lucy Ellen, and to Tom

Published by Monarch Books
an imprint of
Lion Hudson plc
Wilkinson House, Jordan Hill Road,
Oxford OX2 8DR, England
Email: monarch@lionhudson.com
www.lionhudson.com/monarch

ISBN 978 0 85721 655 7
e-ISBN 978 0 85721 656 4

First edition 2015

Acknowledgments
Unless otherwise indicated, Scripture
quotations taken from the Holy Bible, New
International Version Anglicised. Copyright
© 1979, 1984, 2011 Biblica, formerly
International Bible Society. Used by permission
of Hodder & Stoughton Ltd, an Hachette
UK company. All rights reserved. "NIV" is a
registered trademark of Biblica. UK trademark
number 1448790.
Scripture quotations marked "CJB" are taken
from the Complete Jewish Bible. Copyright ©
1998 by David H. Stern. All rights reserved.
Scripture quotations marked "NLT" are taken
from The Holy Bible. New Living Translation
copyright© 1996, 2004, 2007, 2013 by Tyndale
House Foundation. Used by permission of
Tyndale House Publishers Inc., Carol Stream,
Illinois 60188. All rights reserved.
Scripture quotations marked "ASV" are taken
from the American Standard Version, which is
in the public domain.
Scripture quotations marked "ESV" are taken
from The Holy Bible, English Standard Version
Copyright © 2001 by Crossway Bibles, a
publishing ministry of Good News Publishers.
Scripture quotations marked "NASB" are
taken from the New American Standard Bible
(NASB) Copyright © 1960, 1962, 1963, 1968,
1971, 1972, 1973, 1975, 1977, 1995 by The
Lockman Foundation.
Scripture quotations marked "NKJV" are
taken from the New King James Version®.
Copyright © 1982 by Thomas Nelson. Used by
permission. All rights reserved.
Scripture quotations marked "MSG" are
taken from The Message, copyright © 1993,
1994, 1995, 1996, 2000, 2001, 2002. Used by
permission of NavPress Publishing Group.
Scripture quotations from the Authorized
(King James) Version: rights in the Authorized
Version in the United Kingdom are vested in
the Crown. Reproduced by permission of the
Crown's patentee, Cambridge University Press.
Scripture quotations marked "ISV" are taken
from the International Standard Version.
Copyright © 1995–2014 by ISV Foundation.
All rights reserved internationally. Used by
permission of Davidson Press, LLC.

A catalogue record for this book is
available from the British Library

Printed and bound in the UK, May
2016, LH26

Contents

Foreword

A book that traces pathways of hope within dementia, and through dementia care, deserves a warm reception, and this latest book by Louise Morse is worthy of a particularly wide welcome. We are probably all familiar with the African saying that "it takes a village to raise a child". Perhaps, in the light of Louise's observations, we need an additional saying to remind us that "it takes a community to sustain dementia care".

There are many existing supportive communities, friends, families, and churches, and all have a great deal of supportive potential. The joy of Louise Morse's practical approach is that that potential can now be realized to the benefit of those with dementia.

All too often, dementia care rests heavily on the shoulders of a single caregiver who may feel unsupported and at times undermined. The challenges of the task can be great and the last thing a caregiver needs is to feel misunderstood and unappreciated. Even when the lack of understanding centres on the person to whom care is being given, the carer's sense of isolation can increase. And the kind of help that comes with an "I can do better than you" label is certainly of no real help at all. Supportive partnerships are what count.

Twenty years ago it was rewarding for me to share my mother's care when she was in the late stages of dementia. She was struggling to obtain care from her care home staff and the little things I managed to do made a huge difference. It was not just me and the care home, either. The church I was pastoring at the time was a great help too. Sunday by Sunday, church members made Mum feel at home and found undemanding ways of engaging her in conversation. Since those days many aspects of dementia care have been transformed, yet far more can still be done to surround the "cared-for" and the carer with much-needed encouragement.

In my work as President of Churches in Communities International, "community" is a real focus for me. In addition, given my current role as the Free Churches Moderator, healthcare chaplaincy is also on my agenda, being a significant part of the Free Churches' brief within both England and Wales. There are sections of this book that helpfully bring community and chaplaincy together to forge a real pathway of hope, giving us a clear road ahead that we would do well to follow.

Community chaplaincy, in terms of dementia care, may seem a long way off, but it can begin in the local church with a concerned member helping his or her congregation to become dementia-embracing. As the church is awakened to the needs around it, and opens its heart and doors, care can spread into the community. The closed doors in our neighbourhoods may be closed only for want of sensitive visitors and considerate supporters. Fortunately, "sensitive" and "considerate" are the key words that this book is designed to bring into our vocabulary. We now have a great resource in our hands to equip us.

Community, of course, is not the only thread that runs through this book and what is written here will prove invaluable at many levels. I have found much in the book that speaks to my responsibilities and I know you will find much that speaks to yours. We all need hope, and those who need it most will, in their frailty, respond to it more than many of us would expect.

It is my hope that this book will inspire you to have hope and to become a hope-bringer. Please read it with hope in mind.

Revd Dr Hugh Osgood
President of Churches in Communities International
Free Churches Moderator

Acknowledgments

It wouldn't have been possible to write this book without the generosity of the researchers and medical professionals who've published papers and shared their findings either in print or on their websites. I'm especially grateful to those who replied to my emails and questions with patience and clarity and who took time out to talk to me. Cures for Alzheimer's disease or vascular dementia still seem far off but these dedicated researchers will find them at some point. Equally important are those looking to prevent the conditions in the first place, because, as an American physician wrote, "A spoonful of prevention is worth a truck load of cure." A big thank you, then, to the members of this largely unseen army. They all deserve more funding and wider acknowledgment.

I'm also grateful to the people who've shared their experience of the dementia journey, including those who helped in my Master's research and others I've met in the course of my work. It's from years of immersion in this work with a Christian charity that I've learnt so much about older people and different aspects of old age. I'm grateful for the contributions of those at the sharp end – the home managers and nurses, care staff and residents, relatives and volunteers, as well as people at conferences and in churches. They have been incredibly rich sources of experience and learning: they have allowed me to draw from their depths for my first books and then when they were published said how good they were! I've been borne along by their encouragement and appreciation. And right up to the present, I owe a big thank you to my publisher, Tony Collins, who cheers me on in the same way.

Greece is in the news at the moment for all the wrong reasons, but this book owes much to its famous philosopher, Socrates. Socratic thinking is the engine, so to speak, of cognitive behavioural therapy (CBT), the questioning approach that peels away obfuscating layers to reveal the heart of the issue. It has helped not only in understanding people on the dementia journey, but in piercing the morass of information and political spin that surrounds dementia in the media today. An example is the news headline that scientists have identified a blood marker that can show the risk of Alzheimer's disease years before it becomes apparent, but closer reading of the story shows it is referring to a blood protein that's found where there is mild cognitive impairment (MCI). Recent studies show that most people with MCI do not go on to develop dementia, as was previously thought, and the blood marker *may* indicate risk. But so do other conditions, such as chronic stress and depression, and loneliness. Loneliness is so clearly a factor that an Oxford professor wonders why the Government doesn't take steps to address it.

Drawing information from so many sources wouldn't be possible without the internet and the technology that we use to access it. We take so much for granted nowadays, but I owe a big thank you to Dudley, my IT support wizard. From frozen digital phones to blown surge protectors to stuttering computers and disappearing documents, he's quietly rescued me for years, and he's even stopped muttering "operator error" under his breath.

In his book *Outliers* Malcolm Gladwell describes how each individual's achievements are the result of a confluence of influences and opportunities during the person's lifetime. The Bible puts it as people shaping people (Proverbs 27:17), and God opening doors (Proverbs 16:9). Some people reading this book may recognize their contribution while others may not see it – but nevertheless, have been part of the confluence that's led to this book today.

https://www.facebook.com/louise.morse
https://www.facebook.com/pages/Dementia-Books-Louise-Morse
https://www.facebook.com/pages/Pilgrims-Friend-Society
https://twitter.com/Morselouise

Chapter 1
At the Heart of the Matter

The effects of negative thinking

> *Above everything else, guard your heart; for it is the*
> *source of life's consequences. (Proverbs 4:23, CJB)*

It may seem strange to talk about pathways to hope in the context of dementia. Although much more is known about the condition than when I first began writing about it, it still evokes dread and fear, probably more than any other illness. Mention dementia in a group of people and watch their expressions: you can see that it brings up the very worst sort of images – of people in the final stages of the disease, and usually the most severe cases; worst-case scenarios dominate their reactions and feelings.

It's amazing how the human brain seems to grip the most negative and fearful thoughts, outweighing or even ignoring the others, and the hardest battle people have to fight in their minds is the negative thinking that often dismisses all evidence to the contrary. I've seen it in a beautiful young lady who was convinced she was ugly, in an intelligent anorexic who starved herself because she thought she was fat, and in a highly qualified engineer who, despite his string of achievements, was physically affected by high levels of stress because he thought it was all down to luck: in his heart he felt he wasn't good enough. I see it, too, in people's perception of the dementia journey, even among some medical professionals: a nihilistic view that comes from a narrow focus.

The pathway to hope in cognitive behavioural therapy (CBT) is the same as the scripture verse in John 8:32 that says, "You shall know the truth, and the truth shall set you free." CBT is strongly evidence-based; it looks for the facts of the matter. When we examine *all* the evidence in stressful situations we gain an overall perspective that shows us the truth. An example was Eleanor, a retired English teacher who wanted to help immigrants learn English in a programme organized by her church and local Social Services, but who was held back by deep-seated shyness and a tendency to leap to catastrophic conclusions. Teaching was a role with a clear structure and she loved children, but interacting with adults socially was something else altogether. She had been a solitary person for most of her life, but now she really did want to help the immigrants.

Her therapy included changing her behaviour in some challenging circumstances, for instance, joining a table where there were others she didn't know, instead of sitting with a "safe" few, and, importantly, learning to challenge her negative thinking by examining the entire evidence for and against her conclusions, in given situations. The behaviour "experiments" brought responses from others that she hadn't expected, showing her that she was valued and not despised, but her "Aha!" moment came when reading out loud a line on her thought-challenging record. Her daughter-in-law had complained that her husband's study was a real mess, and in a flash Eleanor's thinking had gone from dismay at her daughter-in-law's reaction to fear that she would divorce her son and a conclusion that, without her, the son would end up homeless on the streets. The truth was there was no evidence to support her feelings either in the social situation or about her son's marriage, and seeing that, repeated many times in other instances, set her free.

What has this got to do with pathways to hope in dementia?

In all my conversations and interviews over the years with those whose lives were affected in one way or another by dementia, a frequent theme has been that negative, dysfunctional thinking has skewed perception so that understanding is clouded and important parts of the picture are hidden.

It's particularly pernicious when it comes to family caregivers, whose health can be terribly badly affected by dementia caregiver syndrome (or burden). Caregivers, especially elderly spouses, are known to be likely to develop cardiovascular disease, diabetes, suppressed immune response, raised blood pressure, and more as a result of caregiver burden. In older spouses, it can lead to early death, often before that of the person they are caring for.

Yet research shows this syndrome/burden to be *subjective*, that is, something that springs from negative emotional responses. While the practical and physical aspects of caregiving can of course be demanding, it is not the "objective load" imposed by the care recipient that directly determines burden levels, but its subjective interpretation by the caregiver, and their subsequent ability to cope.

The question I answered in my Master's dissertation was "Can CBT mitigate dementia caregiver burden?", and the answer is, yes, it can. I mentioned this on separate occasions to a neurologist and an old-age psychiatrist, and before I'd finished the sentence they were nodding in agreement. I think it's because CBT is basically applied scriptural common sense. (My college class got used to my saying that this or that CBT concept was written in the Bible thousands of years ago.)

Scriptural precepts really do work. Consider the wisdom of Proverbs 4:23, which tells us to "keep [our] heart with all vigilance, for from it flow the springs of life". The version in the Complete Jewish Bible is even better: "Above everything else, guard your heart; for it is the source of life's consequences."

When we are in stressful situations our minds narrow their focus to deal with the challenges we're facing. We lose our peripheral mental vision and fail to see other factors. That's why we need other people whose vision hasn't narrowed, and who can see the wider picture: it's why two are better than one (Ecclesiastes 4:9–12).

Recently, a couple in their late seventies stopped to talk at a conference where my books on dementia were on display. The wife asked which one might help her best, because her husband had been diagnosed with vascular dementia, and she was not very good at caring for him. She looked an anxious little lady.

"Is that true?" I asked him with a smile.

"No, not at all," he said, smiling back. "She's very good at caring for me."

"Did you hear that?" I asked.

"Yes, but he would say that, wouldn't he?" she answered. Her feeling was so strong she took it to be fact, ignoring the evidence.

I asked, "Would you say you are doing the best you can?"

"Oh yes, I am," she replied, nodding her head, "I am."

"Does God expect anyone to do more than their best?" I asked, and she thought about it before replying, "No, He doesn't, because no one can do more than their best."

"You are doing your best, and God knows that you can't do more than that," I reflected back to her. Then I told her how every caregiver feels inadequate, because there is no training for dementia care and no template, because each case is different: a mixture of the pathology – the disease – and the personality of the individual. It's a journey through unknown territory, and the most important aspect of care is the love the caregiver has for the person with dementia.

"I've never thought of it that way" she said thoughtfully. Then she added a little sentence that spoke volumes: "My brother always said I was behind in catching up." (The sort of brother, I thought, that might have benefited from a clip round the ear.) This time, for the moment at least, she had "caught up" and seen how important the love she felt for her husband was in her care of him, and that God, who sees everything, approved of her doing her best.

The aim of this book is to help give understanding and point out the pathways to hope. And also to tell the stories of people who have found hope – and even joy – in lives touched by dementia.

Chapter 2

The Brightest Hope on the Narrowest Path

The solid nature of real hope, and examples of how it works

> *Your word is a lamp to my feet*
> *and a light to my path. (Psalm 119:105, ESV)*

What do we mean by "hope"? It's a term used in a kind of aspirational way today to mean wishing for an outcome; looking forward to something that may or may not be fulfilled. But "hope" in the biblical sense means more than wishing that something *might* happen; it's a kind of confident expectation, of looking forward to something that we know *will* happen, because God is in it. There are graphic examples of this in my church in Wales.

They are the people who come in from a drug rehabilitation centre. They generally sit together, in the same section of the auditorium. They are mainly men, in their twenties and thirties, all dressed respectably, and they don't just sit there. They're all engaged, and they nearly all worship. Looking at them blesses my socks off. These are people with unimaginably sad backgrounds: former drug addicts, alcoholics, some jailbirds and criminals, yet here they are being loved and accepted and prepared for a new life. It's not a flash-in-the-pan programme, either, which drops them afterwards to make their own way. Some will complete the programme and return to their own regions (I've heard Northern Irish and London accents), but some will stay and become part of the church community.

One of our pastors could never have imagined, when he was a drug addict in prison, that he would go to Bible school and then lead a Pentecostal church, preaching brilliant sermons. His talks on God's "I am" declaration reveal the grand swoop of this God who created the entire universe and yet works in each one of us at atomic level.

Sitting next to a large, leather-jacketed man with a London accent in the foyer one day, I asked what he planned to do next. I thought that he resembled one of the infamous Kray brothers, only bigger and better-looking. He told me he was looking at different work options, but couldn't wait to become part of a team reaching out to people on the streets and in the pubs.

"I want to tell them there's a better way – there's a better future," he said. "The answer is Jesus."

It's important, because how we see the future affects how we feel about our life today. Think about it. How often have you stuck at a tiring or dreary task because the result would be worth it? Jacob worked for his Uncle Laban for fourteen years despite being tricked by him, because he saw a future with his beloved Rachel. If we feel the future is promising, we will work hard towards it.

When he was twelve years of age, Bill Wilson's future was desperately uncertain. He was abandoned on a street corner by his mother, who told him to wait. He stayed on that corner for three days, with no food and no water, waiting for her to come back. Thousands of people passed him by; a small, twelve-year-old boy totally alone and bewildered. On the third day a Christian man stopped to question him, and took him into his own home. He also took him to church and paid for him to go to a Christian summer camp. Bill gave his life to Jesus and for the last thirty-odd years has devoted it to leading thousands of disadvantaged children and youngsters to Christ, and giving them a future. ("Disadvantaged" is putting it mildly.) Now, Bill Wilson's Metro Ministries in New York reach an estimated 30,000 children each week.

It is incredibly tough work. Bill has been stabbed, beaten with baseball bats, and shot in the face; his heart has been broken countless times by the tragedies he sees there. When he spoke at my church he described taking a funeral for a six-year-old child who had been beaten to death by his drug-addicted mother. Not a single family member or friend came to the child's funeral.

In the run-up to Christmas 2013, Bill gave up some of his precious time to be interviewed by Fox News. He was raising money for toys for the thousands of children who would have none that Christmas. The interviewer asked him where he found the strength within himself to move forward, to keep going, and not to become bitter after being abandoned by his mother as a child. He replied that everyone in life has the opportunity to become bitter because of what life throws at us, but added, "I learned that my commitment had to be stronger than my emotions. There will always be something in life that will come at you and so you decide... I believe in who Jesus is. I heard the message; I believed it. I was twelve years old. Looking back, in retrospect, that's what's carried me."[1]

"That's what carried me." Note that Bill didn't say, "That's what I hang on to." Sometimes life is so overwhelming that we can't hang on in our own strength: that's why Jesus hangs on to us. The former drug users and jailbirds at church will tell you the same. The message that they heard and which has carried them has been the *hope* of the message made real by the Holy Spirit within them. It's not a wishy-washy dreamy kind of hope; it has *substance*. It's this that makes the difference in our lives, even when there's dementia. God hangs on to us.

Before the event at Calvary that changed the future for all mankind, Jesus prepared His disciples. He reassured them that they wouldn't be left desolate without Him. He would ask the Father to give them "one who will never leave you. He is the Holy Spirit, who leads into all truth. The world cannot receive him, because it isn't looking for him and doesn't recognize him. But you know him, because he lives with you now and later will be in you" (John 14:16–17, NLT). This is an amazing statement. The Holy Spirit was living with them because Jesus was there, but after He had left earth, His Spirit would live *in* them.

The Holy Spirit is "Christ in us, the hope of glory" (Colossians 1:27, ASV). To the Christians at Colossae the apostle Paul wrote, "This is the secret: Christ lives in you. This gives you assurance of sharing His glory." He is a kind of pledge, a down payment or foretaste of what's to come. He is "God's guarantee that he will give us the inheritance He promised and that He has purchased us to be His own people," (Ephesians 1:14, NLT). Knowing the Holy Spirit is sensing the future, not just wishing for it.

How does this work in dementia?

For some years now, my work has been with a Christian charity founded in 1807 to care for older people. In the early days it helped with regular pensions and practical gifts, such as warm blankets, coal, and groceries. But everything was delivered in person so that there would always be companionship and warm, spiritual support. Nowadays the charity, the Pilgrims' Friend Society (PFS), helps with housing and with nursing and care homes, and by sharing its experience and knowledge with others involved with older people. When I first came on board there were only a few people with dementia in the homes, but now there are dozens, perhaps as many as 50 or 60 per cent. A large part of my work as media and communications manager is meeting and listening to older people and their families and friends, as well as our care home staff and colleagues, and I can't begin to count how many people that means altogether.

In most churches there are now more older people than younger and many pastors are having to deal with issues of old age that they are not familiar with, including dementia, so we are invited, more and more, to talk to churches and Christian organizations. We also take seminars and workshops at national conferences and events. "We" means a small team of people with a similar background of knowledge of different aspects of old age.

When we give talks at national events, if there is a "marketplace" we will have a stand with information about our charity work. Hundreds of people come to us with all sorts of comments and questions. They also send us emails, some staying in touch during their dementia journey. So we are in the middle of a stream of information coming from the "cutting edge", including people who are coping with dementia. It means that as well as academic studies and research our work benefits from a rich stream of personal, current experience, which helps inform all we do.

* * *

Sometimes it helps if we can take a "helicopter view" of our circumstances. When I give talks on dementia I often have a PowerPoint slide that shows a simple continuum:

A   B   C

Point A, on the left, is the time of a person's birth, and point B, on the right, is the year that they developed dementia – way along the line because most cases of dementia occur after the age of seventy. Point C is the time of death, but the Christian's lifeline goes beyond that into eternity, to "infinity and beyond", where there's heaven, then the new earth and the new heaven. It's difficult to draw "infinity and beyond" on a book page, but I hope you can see what I mean. So, speaking very generally, for most of our lives we're more or less OK and then, when we're older (as a rule), we can develop dementia. Looked at in the light of eternity, dementia can be said to fall into the category of "light momentary affliction" that the apostle Paul describes when recounting the things he suffered (2 Corinthians 4:17, ESV).

Our lives now are just a prelude to something bigger, better, and more glorious than we can ever imagine. Look up 1 Corinthians 2:9–10 and read it slowly, savouring the sure hope in the words. I love the way *The Message* puts it:

No one's ever seen or heard anything like this,
Never so much as imagined anything quite like it –
What God has arranged for those who love him.

But you've *seen and heard it because God by his*
Spirit has brought it all out into the open before you.

It resonates within us, this hope of glory. Paul, a pastor in his seventies, was devastated when his beloved wife, Lillian, developed Lewy body dementia. He was determined to take care of her at home until his own health began to give way and he was persuaded to arrange respite care for her in a home near where they lived. Before a week was out, he had brought her home. She'd become so dehydrated that their family doctor warned she might not live another twenty-four hours unless he could "get fluids into her". The care home had sedated her as a way of coping with her frequent, rapid walking. She was so sedated that she couldn't stand, and wasn't able to take in sufficient fluid. (Not all care homes are like this, and most have good standards.) A fellow pastor recommended our Pilgrim Home in Evington, Leicester, and Paul made a round trip of ninety miles two or three times a week to be with her. He said he was able to drive home in peace, knowing that she was being loved and cared for. Lillian had helped to build their church, he told me. When he spoke about all she had done in her lifetime, it was like listening to the account of the excellent woman in Proverbs. Facing life without her was like having a major amputation, such was his grief. But when we touched on the life that is to come, when she will be better than she's ever been before and they will be together again, his face lit up like the midday sun. It isn't something that he imagines or has wishy-washy hopes for; it's the Holy Spirit within him saying, "Yes, this is how it will be!" And at the same time he was ministering in the home, taking daily services and bringing hope to others. A pastor's heart never switches off, it seems. He was a special encouragement to other residents and staff.

My colleague Janet has seen the difference that this "hope of glory" makes. At a national event she met two couples, for whom there had been a diagnosis of dementia. The first couple were in their sixties, and the wife had been told she had Alzheimer's. They talked to Janet about what it meant to them, but above all, the wife said, they had come to terms with it, and were making plans for their future.

Coming to terms with it included thanking God for all He'd done in their lives. They had counted their blessings, well and truly. They were not in denial, because they knew what lay ahead, but they were determined to wring the most enjoyment out of the life they had left.

"We know that Alzheimer's is terminal," she said. "But we've got all the information and we've told our family and friends what to expect. What's the point in worrying about it? It doesn't change anything, does it? Best of all, we know that this is not the end for us. We believe in Jesus: we're looking forward to the new heaven and the new earth." She picked up a copy of my book *Could It Be Dementia? Losing Your Mind Doesn't Mean Losing Your Soul*, and, pointing to the title, said to her husband, "That's it!"

At the same conference was another couple where the wife had been diagnosed with dementia. Janet said that they were both in their late sixties, but looked more like eighty-year-olds. Seeing them put her in mind of Atlas, carrying the world on his shoulders.

"They were bent over and looked so weighed down," she said. They were very angry with God.

"We had so many plans for our retirement, and now they're all shattered," they said. Janet tried to reassure them, telling them that there are often good years of life after diagnosis, and encouraging them to get involved in their church fellowship. She felt the weight of their depression, and after they'd gone prayed for them on and off during the day, and then for about a year. She remembers feeling "a real burden" for them.

To her surprise, the next year the same couple came to the stand again.

"Do you remember us?" they asked.

"Oh I do," she replied. "I've been praying for you for a full year!" She said they looked quite different. Their expressions were lighter and they were even standing up straighter. They told her they'd come to terms with everything; that the Lord knew all about it and they were leaning on Him. Yes, they were walking through the valley of the shadow, but they felt His presence with them. Most of all, they were taking the helicopter view, looking into eternity. There are many stories like theirs in the following chapters.

If you are living with Jesus Christ you are on the "The Road of Blessing", as one of my favourite authors, Penelope Wilcock, puts it.[2] As she says, it's a road you can step on to, whoever and wherever you are. "But though it doesn't matter where you join the road or how you make a start, it matters very much that you do actually begin." It's very simple to step on to the road of blessing; you tell Jesus that you need Him to be your Saviour, and ask Him into your life. He's the Door. He never turns anyone away and it is never too late.

Jesus said that this road of blessing, this pathway, is narrow (Matthew 7:13, 14). It has a constant, close focus on Him – it has to, because He is the way, the truth, and the life (John 14:6, KJV). And, as we've heard, the glorious thing is that He gives us His Holy Spirit to guide and comfort us.

This is our main shining hope, our hope of glory. This hope lights up our lives, lights up our hearts, illuminates our thinking, and chases away dark shadows. In its light we see pathways to hope in dementia. Some are highways through the heart and some are practical things to do. We'll be looking at these in the following chapters, with real-life examples that show how they "work".

Notes

1. https://www.youtube.com/watch?v=3KxM-aFjYoQ
2. Penelope Wilcock, *The Road of Blessing*, Oxford: Monarch 2011.

Chapter 3

Understanding Dementia and Finding Pathways to Hope

What dementia is, what it isn't, and the importance of resilience

> *I praise you, for I am fearfully and wonderfully made.*
> *Wonderful are your works; my soul knows it very well*
> *(Psalm 139:14, ESV)*

Max Pemberton is a hospital doctor with an interest in dementia. He writes books and columns in national newspapers. In an internet trawl recently he came across an advertisement that featured a host of celebrities, one which he said was "one of the most star-studded commercials of all… It featured a former nurse who has been diagnosed with the disease. It made me realize how far we, as a nation, have come in the past decade or so. When I was training to be a doctor, no one – and certainly not celebrities – wanted to talk about dementia. Even doctors rarely spoke about it and it was considered a Cinderella speciality. Well not any more."

Yes, this Cinderella made it to the ball and is under the spotlight. But, like the heroine in the fairy tale, it is widely seen but not understood; in fact, more often than not it is misunderstood. We are often asked, still, if Alzheimer's is the same as dementia. "My relative has been diagnosed with Alzheimer's," we are often asked, "so does it mean she will get dementia?" Even professionals who might be expected to understand dementia often don't, caregivers tell us.

"None of them seemed to understand my mother," said a bereaved daughter, "not the social workers, not the doctor, not the consultant; nobody."

If it's possible to shout on Facebook, that's what a wife did after her husband had died. She wrote, "Silence is the worst thing! Silence (in the media and the world 'at large') is the reason I knew nothing of this subject, and so failed to spot the early symptoms in my husband. Silence, and lack of knowledge, is why me, my husband, and my kids, hit wall after wall of difficulties and needless hurt, of bureaucratic ignorance, battles with Social Services, with the NHS... I could go on. But... the bottom line is... dementia needs to come out in the open, as an illness, better discussed, experiences and knowledge shared… for everyone's benefit, because this is a problem which is on the rise."

But we push away from us things we would rather not have near us, and who is interested in reading about dementia until it affects their life? Also, as I mentioned earlier, because it's a combination of the pathology and the personality, it manifests differently with every person. Clinical psychologist Graham Stokes sums it up in his question, "If the signs and symptoms of dementia are the direct result of the brain pathology, why are they [those affected] not all compliant and quiet, or noisy and aggressive? How is it that... some maintain their daily living skills far longer than others?"[1] There's a hidden hope in this question, and we take a longer look at this later in the chapter.

In the meantime: what is dementia?

It's a Latin word that means, literally, "apart from" or "away from the mind". It's not a description of the disease itself but of the symptoms. There are said to be around 100 different causes of dementia, but in the simplest terms dementia results from physical damage to the brain. The term "dementia" could become outdated if the updated DSM, *The Diagnostic and Statistical Manual of Mental Disorders* (dubbed "The Psychiatrist's Bible"), has its way. The latest edition lists dementia as a neurological disorder and replaces the term "dementia" with "major neurocognitive disorder and mild neurocognitive disorder". The authors acknowledge, though, that healthcare professionals are likely to use the shorter label, "dementia". However, listing the disease as a neurocognitive disorder acknowledges its physiological origin. American health and fitness author Porter Shimer believes that it's important to recognize that dementia is a physical, medical condition. Noting that dementia means "away from the mind", he writes, "It's important to remember that this 'going away' has happened for physical reasons in dementia... while the disease can affect behaviour in ways that may appear to reflect psychological instability, the illness is first and foremost a physical one, brought on by the death of brain cells plus a shortage of chemicals (neurotransmitters) needed to keep those cells both active and alive."[2]

The signs of dementia

Neurologist Dr Allan Ropper says that patients present with symptoms and doctors look for signs.[3] Most of the people who talk to us mention "the signs of dementia". The first sign they notice is forgetfulness. I often wonder if they've always been forgetful but because they've reached a certain age and are now in the dementia zone, they are noticing it more. If you're reading this and think this applies to you, you'll be encouraged to know you can train yourself out of it. If you forget where you've put things, it's because your mind has moved on and has gone somewhere else. Is this "flash dementia"? No, it means you're not paying attention. But you can train yourself to "snapshot" the moment, and lay down a clear memory in your mind. Have you gone into another room and forgotten why? Our immediate short-term memory is very easily distractible, says neurologist Dr Oliver Cockerell. "Your brain knows you're unlikely to need to remember a menial task such as going upstairs to get a book in a few hours, so it erases the memory to make room for more important stuff. That's why we all sometimes can't remember why we walked into a room."[4] If I'd known that the reason I'm absent-minded is that my brain is full of more important stuff, I'd have wielded it as a defence to my family.

Two of the earliest signs of dementia are not being able to smell things, and not being able to navigate. A major effort is finding reliable markers for identifying Alzheimer's disease, and it's been suggested that "olfactory dysfunction", or not being able to smell, could be one of them.[5] And often the part of the brain that helps us navigate is among the first to be affected by Alzheimer's. One time I saw an elderly lady completely lose her sense of direction in IKEA's U-shaped meal service lines. But I also know people who have never had a sense of direction. A friend from church could come out of Boots the Chemist and not know which way she needed to turn. The key is not having had these abilities, but having had them and *losing* them.

A Nobel Prize has been awarded to scientists who discovered the group of cells in the brain that are responsible for our GPS system, making it possible for our brains to work out where we are.[6] If they could translate it into a technology for map reading, they would make a fortune, because although maps show you the place you want to reach they don't tell you where you are, which explains why they have to be turned around and upside down.

However, in patients with Alzheimer's disease, the area of the brain that helps with navigation is often affected at an early stage. The husband in Frank and Linda's story (a true story of a couple's journey with dementia) is a prime example. The opening chapter begins with Frank insisting that Linda reverse the car into their next-door neighbour's driveway, which he sees as their own. Once an excellent driver and navigator, Frank could no longer find his way home even on familiar routes that he'd driven for years. Often he didn't recognize where they were – hence the neighbour's driveway. Retired old-age psychiatrist Dr Daphne Wallace tells how she knew for sure there was something seriously wrong when she lost her way driving over Dartmoor. She had always been a superb navigator.

Temporary, treatable dementias

Before looking at definitions of the main dementias, it's worth looking at other conditions that can cause dementia, but are treatable. There's a whole range of causes, and older people seem to be particularly vulnerable. These causes include vitamin deficiencies (particularly B1 and B12), reactions to drugs, hormonal imbalances, anaemia, urinary tract infections, brain tumours, underactive thyroid, high fever, and dehydration. Frailty in old age, which can affect both physical and mental performance, can be caused by undetected cardiovascular disease.[7] One of my older relatives was becoming very doddery, physically and mentally, but when her condition was treated the change was noticeable. She didn't seem to be much stronger physically, but her mind was much sharper and she was more her old self. Depression can also produce dementia-like symptoms; in fact, it's sometimes caused a pseudo-dementia. Depression can also reduce blood flow to the brain.[8] Feelings of loneliness can lead to apathy and depression. In a global survey a few years ago, the World Health Organization found that depression was seen as the worst of all disorders. Professor Sarah Pressman, of the University of Kansas, and Gallup did a global survey of 150,000 people in 2009 and were amazed to find that the link between emotion and physical health was *greater than* the association between health and basic human requirements such as food. They presented their findings at the American Psychosomatic Society meeting in Chicago. The Royal College of Psychiatrists has excellent advice for older people with depression.[9]

The cholesterol-lowering drug statin may be responsible for memory loss, according to researchers at the University of California, San Diego. Dr Beatrice Golomb's team has been studying the effects of statins for a number of years, and has presented papers showing that the risks outweigh the benefits for older people, with memory loss a significant factor.[10] Anecdotal evidence from first-hand experiences has been reported in the national press, perhaps most notably by a journalist who found that when taking statins his mind filled with fog and he "lost his words". When he forgot to take the pills on holiday, his memory and mind returned to normal.[11] A vascular surgeon has taken the trouble to write an article giving the reasons he stopped taking statins.[12] Many people find that statins work well for them, but the risk of side effects seems to increase with age.

Mild cognitive impairment

There is also a condition called "mild cognitive impairment" (MCI), which can be seen as a precursor to dementia, but recent studies show that more people revert to normal than go on to develop dementia. A study in November 2014 by the Mayo Clinic[13] showed that "'absolute rates of progression to dementia are… much lower in population-based samples (well below 10%) than in clinic-based samples", adding that "neither the benefits nor the harms of diagnosing MCI at the population level have been rigorously explored. At present, insufficient evidence exists for a beneficial effect of screening for dementia itself". A "well below 10%" progression to dementia in population-based samples is good news.

It's always a good idea to check for physical causes of mental frailty in older people, as well as for stress, feelings of loneliness, and depression.

The signs that it could be dementia

Here come some rather "dry" descriptions of the causes of dementia. If you know them already, you may want to skip to the "Hidden Hope" section, where you'll make some surprising discoveries.

Alzheimer's disease is the biggest cause of dementia, accounting for around 60 per cent of cases. In Alzheimer's disease, brain cells are destroyed by amyloid plaques. "Amyloid" is a general term for protein fragments that the body produces normally. In a healthy brain, these plaques are broken down and eliminated, but, in Alzheimer's, the fragments accumulate to form hard, insoluble plaques that damage the structure of the neurones. Some recent studies suggest that a good night's sleep could help these deposits drain away.[14] Another has discovered that a single protein may inhibit the brain's natural hoovering-up system. They found that blocking the protein in mice with a drug reversed memory loss and myriad other Alzheimer's-like features in the animals.[15]

Vascular dementia is the second most common form of dementia and is caused by reduced blood flow to the brain – usually from a stroke or series of strokes. While the strokes may be unnoticeably small, the damage can add up over time, leading to memory loss, confusion, and other signs of dementia. While there is no known cure, you can learn to manage symptoms, prevent further strokes, and enjoy a full, rewarding life. Next to Alzheimer's, this is the most common cause of dementia, accounting for around 20 per cent. It is often found in combination with Alzheimer's disease.

Lewy body dementia (LBD) is another common form attributed to changes in brain tissue. Lewy bodies are accumulated bits of protein inside the nuclei of neurones in areas of the brain that control particular aspects of memory and motor control. Dementia with Lewy bodies usually occurs sporadically, in people with no known family history of the disease. It is not a single disorder but a spectrum of disorders, including dementia with Lewy bodies (DLB) and Parkinson's disease dementia (PDD). Early and accurate diagnosis is important, as LBD patients may respond differently from Alzheimer's disease patients to certain dementia and behavioural treatments.

Fronto-temporal lobe dementia (FTD) is an umbrella term for a diverse group of rare disorders that primarily affect the frontal and temporal lobes of the brain – the areas generally associated with judgment, inhibition, and behaviour. In FTD, portions of these lobes atrophy, or shrink. FTD is often misdiagnosed as a psychiatric problem or as Alzheimer's disease. But it tends to occur at a younger age than does Alzheimer's disease, typically between the ages of forty and seventy. The memory problems associated with Alzheimer's disease are not as prominent in the early stages of FTD. Symptoms vary: some people with FTD undergo dramatic changes in their personality and become socially inappropriate, impulsive, or emotionally blunted, while others lose the ability to use and understand language.

Posterior cortical atrophy was made famous, sadly, when author Terry Pratchett announced that he had been diagnosed with it after experiencing a succession of what he called "Clapham Junction days". Sir Terry was a wordsmith par excellence, skilled with a keyboard and used to working with six PC monitors.

He said, "For me, things came to a head in the late summer of 2007. My typing had been getting progressively worse and my spelling had become erratic. I grew to recognize what I came to call Clapham Junction days when the demands of the office grew too much to deal with."[16] His medical examinations were challenging because his capacity for words was extraordinarily large. He was articulate and could easily remember the three key words. But at a reading of his latest book at the annual Terry Pratchett Day, he could manage only a few lines before the part of his brain that should have been recognizing words seemed to shut down.

Posterior cortical atrophy is most usually considered to be an unusual or atypical variant of Alzheimer's disease, though it tends to affect people at an earlier age. It is a progressive degenerative condition involving the loss and dysfunction of brain cells particularly at the back (posterior) of the brain. In most cases, this loss of brain cells is associated with the same pathology seen in typical Alzheimer's disease, that is, amyloid plaques and neurofibrillary tangles. Sufferers tend to have well-preserved memory and language but instead show a progressive, dramatic, and relatively selective decline in vision and/or literacy skills such as spelling, writing, and arithmetic.

Wernicke–Korsakoff syndrome is a disorder involving the loss of specific brain functions caused by a thiamine deficiency. The main cause is long-term alcohol misuse, which can lead to poor absorption and storage of thiamine. Complications include permanent loss of memory, permanent loss of cognitive skills, and difficulties with social and personal interaction. Careers, relationships, and social lives are often severely affected.

There may also be symptoms of uncoordinated walking and confusion, disturbed vision, and hallucinations. Heavy alcohol use interferes with the breakdown of thiamine in the body, so even if someone with alcoholism follows a well-balanced diet, most of the thiamine is not absorbed. There is damage to multiple nerves in both the central nervous system (brain and spinal cord) and the peripheral nervous system (the rest of the body). The initial physical symptoms include abnormal gait and eye movements. Less commonly, the syndrome is not caused by alcohol abuse but follows nutritional stress such as rapid weight loss, bowel obstruction, thyrotoxicosis, cancer, or renal dialysis.

Other causes of dementia can include AIDS, hydrocephalus, systemic lupus erythematosus, Lyme disease, hypercalcemia, multiple sclerosis, or diseases such as Parkinson's, Creutzfeldt–Jakob, and Huntington's. Dementia can also result from a head injury that causes haemorrhaging in the brain, or from a reaction to a medication.

It's worth reminding ourselves again that, whatever the diagnosis, however changed the person's behaviour as the condition progresses, the essence of the person and their core values do not change. One of a bereaved wife's treasures is a snapshot taken by care home staff of her and her husband, standing underneath a sunshade at a garden party. Looking frail and lost, he is leaning towards her, taking comfort in her presence, their arms loosely around each other.

"He didn't know who I was at that time," she said, "but he was distressed at being outside with all the others, with all the noise and activity. It's something he would have hated." She had drawn him aside into the relative seclusion under the shade, apart from the rest. Care home staff wouldn't have known that. In another home a very shy man, who hated being in the lounge with everyone else and who loved being outside in the garden, broke the glass patio doors to get outside. Knowing the person is so important.

The hidden hope

Scientists are still working to understand how the brain works – this 1.5 kg of putty-like matter which is the most complex biological structure on earth. Some of the most intriguing findings from studies in dementia research get very little public attention, perhaps because they don't have a springboard for further research or for pharmaceutical development. One is known as the Nun Study, a longitudinal study started in 1986 by David Snowdon at the University of Minnesota to examine the effects of ageing on the brain and the onset of dementia. Nearly 700 retired nuns from the School Sisters of Notre Dame, Mankato, took part. They were ideal for scientific study because their stable, relatively similar lives precluded a number of factors that could contribute to illness. They didn't smoke, drank little, if any alcohol, and ate in convent cafeterias, and most had been teachers in Catholic schools. Dr Snowdon's condition that the nuns donate their brains for research after death was a stumbling block for some of the sisters, but Sister Rita Schwalbe, the convent's health administrator when the study began, said that as nuns they had made "the difficult decision not to have children. This is another way of giving life". For fifteen years the nuns' genes were analysed and they were tested on a range of physical and mental exercises, such as their strength and ability to balance, how many words they could remember minutes after reading them on flashcards, how many animals they could name in a minute, and whether they could count coins correctly. The autobiographical essays they wrote for their order in their twenties, when they took their vows, were scrutinized, and their words plumbed for meaning. After they died, their brains were removed and shipped to a laboratory, where they were autopsied. Among the findings were that early language ability may be linked to a lower risk of Alzheimer's because nuns who packed more ideas into the sentences of their early autobiographies were less likely to get Alzheimer's disease six decades later, and that nuns who expressed more positive emotions in their autobiographies lived significantly longer than those expressing fewer positive emotions.

Perhaps the most surprising finding was that there was very little correlation between neuropathology in the brains of nuns who had exhibited dementia while they were alive and those who had not. In fact, "the correlation between neuropathological lesions and cognition was modest, accounting only for about a quarter of the variance of cognition among older adults. As such, the concept of resilient ageing has emerged in recent years as a useful construct in characterizing such individuals who maintain intact cognitive function amidst evidence of significant AD pathology".[17]

In other words, some of the nuns' brains had all the signs of Alzheimer's disease, but their owners had shown no sign of it while they were alive. In 80 per cent of the cases the pathology did not concur with the symptoms seen during life, and other studies since have showed the same, which is very puzzling, if you think about it. If you break your arm you can't use it until it's been set and healed, and the symptoms and time of healing are more or less the same for everybody. There's a clear link between the damage and the symptoms.

If you have a tumour in a certain part of the brain, neurologists are able to tell you, with some degree of accuracy, how you will be affected. The youngest son of some friends was found to have a tumour deep in his brain, which had caused severe hyperactivity and epilepsy in the years before it was discovered. At one point it was so bad that when he was awake the child could not stop moving. Some days he could eat only by snatching food from a table as he ran up and down a corridor. Neurologists at Great Ormond Street Hospital warned the parents that, although removing the tumour would remove the epilepsy, it was a very delicate operation and there could be some collateral brain damage. My heart sank when they told me this.

"How bad?" I asked.

"He might lose some peripheral vision," they answered with a big smile, because the loss of peripheral vision was nothing compared to the life-threatening effects of the tumour.

Kitwood suggested that individuals may vary considerably in the extent to which they are able to withstand processes in the brain that destroy synapses, and hence in their resistance to dementia. He thought that it could be owing to the "very great differences between human beings in the degree to which nerve architecture has developed as a result of learning and experience".[18]

The authors of *Resilient Brain Aging: Characterization of Discordance between Alzheimer's Disease Pathology and Cognition*[19] look at the resilience that Kitwood implies, while other commentaries suggest that it may be down to having a positive outlook, or the effects of individuals' early socio-economic status. Others are convinced that having good cardiovascular health could explain the discordance. Or could it be the result of a lifetime spent in "cognitively stimulating activity?" asks Dr William Jagust, lead researcher in a UC Berkeley study on how the brain worked in people with, and without, Alzheimer's disease.[20]

Another interesting piece of research was another UC Berkeley study, which involved seventy-one (live) adults of different ages who showed no sign of mental decline. Scans showed that sixteen of the older subjects had amyloid deposits characteristic of Alzheimer's disease, while the remaining fifty-five did not. Each one was given various cognitive tests while his or her brain was tracked by fMRI (functioning magnetic resonance imaging). Everyone performed equally well in the tasks, but researchers saw that, for people with amyloid deposits in the brain, the more detailed and complex their memory (it was a memory recall task), the more active their brains were, with more parts being involved. Dr Jagust observed that, "It seemed that their brain has found a way to compensate for the presence of the proteins associated with Alzheimer's." Their brains were "rewiring" around the obstacles. What remains unclear is why some people's brains are better at doing it than others. Previous studies published by Dr Jagust's team suggested that people who engage in mentally stimulating activities throughout their lives have fewer amyloid deposits, though the study under discussion looked at how the brain found its way around them.

A few hundred of us saw an example of this at a large church conference in Birmingham. One of the speakers was Dr Jennifer Bute, a general practitioner who retired after being diagnosed with dementia at the age of sixty-three. She can describe what it's like to have dementia, and how the brain is able to rewire. She talked about practical matters, such as communicating and the meaning of behaviour, and also said that the spirit of the person is not lost because the person's brain is damaged, but lives for ever. Jennifer has set up a website offering a great deal of information, including a couple of films she has made. It is immensely valuable because she speaks authoritatively as someone with medical insight who is now experiencing dementia. She may be an example of a lifetime spent in "cognitively stimulating activity".

It's well worth visiting her website at www.glorious opportunity.org. When I meet people like Jennifer I tuck them into a mental Rolodex of people whose company I look forward to enjoying when we are part of that "vast congregation" in heaven, and beyond – the new heaven and the new earth. Sometimes I turn that Rolodex slowly and savour the thought of the people and the conversations we'll enjoy in heaven. "Will there be cups of tea in heaven?" I asked one time on Facebook.

Perhaps one of the most striking examples of an active brain rewiring is Christine Bryden, author of two books on dementia, *Who Will I Be When I Die?* and *Dancing with Dementia*. In 1995, Christine was a senior executive in the Australian Prime Minister's Department, heading up the science and technology division, and had been awarded the Public Service Medal in 1994. Her life changed dramatically when she was diagnosed with dementia (she was then forty-six) and she struggled as a single mother with three daughters aged nineteen, fourteen, and nine. She was told that she would need full-time care within five years and would be dead before she turned sixty.[21]

Since then Christine has written two books, spoken at international conferences, remarried, taken a postgraduate degree, and helped found the Dementia Advocacy and Support Network International (DASNI). She helped to establish support groups in Canberra for people newly diagnosed with dementia, and she set up the national Consumer Focus Group, which advises the Australian Alzheimer's Association on policies and programmes. She still speaks at conferences and is now sixty-six years old. In the twenty years since her diagnosis, Christine has done more than most people do in their whole lifetime.

We've kept lightly in touch via email, and recently met here in Wales at the Celtic Manor Resort (famous for hosting the NATO leaders and the Ryder Golf Cup). She and her husband had taken a brief holiday in Wales after speaking engagements in England. A few years ago I'd extracted part of a speech she gave at a DASNI conference and turned it into a poem (it's in Chapter 8), and we were trying to recall where she'd given the talk. She turned to her husband, Paul, but he couldn't remember. She thought a bit, and then said, "I think it was in 2005.'" Christine told me that, when he views her current brain scans, her consultant says she should not be functioning at the level she is. I asked what she thought most contributed to it, and she said, "'The Holy Spirit.'" As far as I know, scientists don't take the Holy Spirit into account when they do their research.

A medical disease model doesn't seem able to join the dots when it comes to dementia. None of us conforms to a standard pattern for anything. The astonishing thing about human beings is that, although there are millions and millions of us on earth, each one is unique. Even identical twins differ in many ways. Taking into account all the human beings that have been born, lived, and died since the first two in the garden of Eden, it is amazing that none have been duplications. Governments can produce trillions of coins and notes but, within their values, they are all identical, every single one. Only God could design something as marvellous and diverse as human beings. Only Someone as majestic as this could make us all in His image, yet give us the freedom to be uniquely individual.

Notes

1. Graham Stokes, *Challenging Behaviour in Dementia: A Person-centred Approach*, London: Speechmark Press, 2000.
2. Porter Shimer, *New Hope for People and their Caregivers*, New York: Prima Publishing (Random House) 2002.
3. Allan Ropper and BD Burrell, *Reaching Down the Rabbit Hole*, London: Atlantic Books, 2014.
4. http://www.dailymail.co.uk/health/article-2989417/Worried-swamping-dementia-clinics-trivial-memory-fears-losing-car-keys-just-absent-minded.html#ixzz3U5Ws9LR1
5. http://www.ncbi.nlm.nih.gov/pmc/articles/PMC3629552
6. http://www.http://timesofindia.indiatimes.com/world/uk/The-discovery-of-a-GPS-system-inside-a-human-brain-that-tells-us-who-we-are/articleshow/44511131.cms theguardian.com/science/2014/oct/06/nobel-prize-physiology-medicine-brain-gps
7. http://www.medscape.com/viewarticle/788770
8. http://www.sciencedaily.com/releases/2007/08/070808132027.htm
9. http://www.rcpsych.ac.uk/healthadvice/problemsdisorders/depressioninolderadults.aspx
10. https://www.youtube.com/watch?v=Q_miCHrRvPg
11. http://www.telegraph.co.uk/health/4974840/Wonder-drug-that-stole-my-memory.html

12. http://www.telegraph.co.uk/health/10717431/Why-Ive-ditched-statins-for-good.html
13. Richard, E. & Brayne, C. *Nature Reviews Neurology* 10, 130–131 (2014); published online 18 February 2014; doi:10.1038/nrneurol.2014.23;
14. http://www.nih.gov/news/health/oct2013/ninds-17.htm
15. http://www.telegraph.co.uk/news/science/science-news/11280504/Has-Stanford-University-found-a-cure-for-Alzheimers-disease.html
16. http://www.dailymail.co.uk/health/article-1070673/Terry-Pratchett-Im-slipping-away-bit-time-I-watch-happen.html#ixzz3NUwoDqGS
17. http://www.ncbi.nlm.nih.gov/pubmed/23919768
18. Kitwood, *Dementia Reconsidered*, OUP, 2008.
19. Curr Alzheimer Res. Oct 2013; 10(8): 844–851.
20. http://newscenter.berkeley.edu/2014/09/14/neural-compensation-for-alzheimers-beta-amyloid
21. http://www.dailymail.co.uk/news/article-2674496/Woman-survived-20-years-dementia-new-love-astonishes-doctors.html

Chapter 4

The Diagnosis Dilemma and the Crossroads

The push for more diagnosis and the lack of care brings us to a crossroads

[... heaven in our hearts]... and who has also put his seal on us and given us his Spirit in our hearts as a guarantee (2 Corinthians 1:22, ESV)

Sometimes, the sense of heaven is strong in elderly Christians. It's as though the walls between this world and that are thinner. A carer, now retired, tells about the time she was sitting with two elderly ladies in one of our homes, helping one to eat and encouraging the other. The conversation went something like this:

Dora (to Gertie): "I've seen you somewhere before."

Gertie: "Have you? I don't remember seeing you."

Dora: "I know your face."

Gertie: "Where did we meet?"

Dora: "When we were on earth."

Gertie: "Oh; where are we now?"

Dora: "In heaven."

Gertie (with tears in her eyes): "I am so glad!"

Then they both stood up and hugged each other.

"A never-to-be-forgotten little scene," wrote the carer. Even though their dementia was advanced enough for them to need residential care, both ladies were so safe and contented that they felt they were in heaven. This is how people with dementia should be cared for. (You can see a short video of the home, taken not so long ago, on YouTube, at https://www.youtube.com/watch?v=I1_K2D6oC08. Please don't think that I'm plugging the charity's homes: I just want you to see how God intended us to care for frail older people.)

The professional film-maker who made this film for us is a partner in a Christian company whose regular work is making sophisticated films for global corporations, often showcasing glamorous or expensive products. They do this for us as part of their tithing, their giving back to the Lord, and have visited a few of our care homes now. In one instance the charge for a day's shoot was so small that I queried it. "I know we're a charity," I said, "but surely, with all the travel and the time and the editing and so on, this must leave you out of pocket." Back came the response that the sum fell within the amount set aside for their tithing, and they didn't want me to "mess with it". Besides, they said, this work was on "holy ground". And they are right. Jesus said that whenever we touch someone who belongs to Him ("my brethren"), we are touching Him (Matthew 25:40). And we are caring for people whose next step is to be before the Lord. We feel very privileged.

Diagnosing dementia can be a dilemma partly because it's not straightforward. Despite technology, it is subjective and down to interpretation. It's also a dilemma because in the UK at the moment it's being conflated with care and support, which is worrying, because it hides the fragile state of our adult social care system. A mid-2014 survey among Directors of Adult Social Services showed that the care system is almost at meltdown, and "unsustainable"' because of an ageing population and an unprecedented squeeze on budgets.[1] Research by charity Age UK found that around 900,000 older people were facing catastrophe because they cannot obtain care.

Knowing that aftercare is not properly available makes the push for more diagnoses deeply puzzling. It began in 2013, when GPs were issued with guidelines from the NHS urging them to screen older patients discreetly when they visited the surgery. It was enough to make anyone aged seventy-five or over nervous about seeing their doctor in case he or she might eye them speculatively. (A seventy-six-year-old we met at a conference told us that he'd gone to his GP with a physical ailment and was annoyed to be asked, out of the blue, how many children he had.) At the time, a group of leading medical professionals told the Government why it would be counter-productive, and recommended that it should not be done.[2] In 2010 the UK National Screening Committee, whose remit is to advise the Government on all screening programmes, had advised very clearly that screening for Alzheimer's disease "should not be offered". But their professional medical opinions were ignored.

Even so, it seemed that discreet screening didn't bring the numbers up enough. About eighteen months later, at the annual meeting of the Royal College of General Practitioners in Liverpool, GPs were offered an incentive of £55 for each newly diagnosed patient. Many protested, pointing out that without adequate aftercare a diagnosis would be harmful: it would cause stress, fear, and uncertainty. The deputy chairman of the General Practitioners' Committee, Dr Richard Vautrey, said the incentive scheme ignored patients' and carers' real needs. "The key focus for NHS England should be providing and ensuring better services for patients that actually have dementia," he said. "That's the area GPs are most concerned about: ensuring that patients and carers get the right amount of support, and that's something that's often lacking. That's where there's a real need for improvement."

Psychogeriatrician Dr Chris Fox (University of East Anglia) was among those warning that sending more patients for referral invited a relatively high risk of misdiagnosis, adding that "it was unfair to cause fear and concern when treatments are not available, the chances of the condition actually progressing are not clear, and when symptoms may never take hold in the patient's lifetime".

* * *

Dementia UK, an organization whose Admiral Nurses specialize in dementia care, stated, "Many good GPs are already doing this [making diagnoses] to support families, but many are hesitant because of the dearth of follow-up care. These plans suggest that we're able to give people a better quality of life if diagnosed much earlier, but that would depend solely on our ability to deliver high-quality post-diagnostic support. The fact is that, as a country, we're not currently delivering this support in a consistent way." Writing in *The Guardian* from personal experience, journalist Rose George said, "I know from my dad's awful experience that dementia care is in trouble. Paying GPs to diagnose won't even begin to fix it." She goes on to describe the "shabby, confusing and often callous system" that still passes for dementia "care".[3]

The Alzheimer's Society website posted in July 2014 an article beginning "Desperate Lack of Support for People with a Dementia Diagnosis".[4] "Too many people are left without a guiding hand to help them come to terms with this debilitating, terminal condition," the article continued. "The Government has shown clear commitment to improving the lives of people with dementia and action is under way to improve diagnosis rates. However, we cannot escape the lack of support following a diagnosis which leaves vulnerable people adrift."

Health Minister Jeremy Hunt also acknowledged the lack of care at a major conference in London, when he called for a "revolution in out-of-hospital care" so that those with dementia got joined-up help and support from community services and GPs. "Britain has a long way to go before it can be fully 'proud' of the way it handles dementia – with half of sufferers left to feel like a burden," he said. Yet, at the same event, he called for an end to "fatalism" about the condition, telling GPs that those with dementia have a "basic human right" to be given a diagnosis.[5] The implication was that nihilistic GPs, in not diagnosing patients, are preventing them from receiving "tailored care and support". Yet eighteen months earlier, responding to a question in Parliament, Mr Hunt had conceded that, "Some GPs... have a point when they are concerned that it is very, very difficult to access good services for people who have dementia. So the way that we will change GPs' minds is for them to appreciate that something will change if someone gets a dementia diagnosis and that is the big challenge that this ministerial team has set the Department."[6] Even after reading several times what he said, it still seems that Mr Hunt is acknowledging that there is little aftercare, but that if GPs make enough diagnoses then it might be put in place. In August 2015, the Royal College of General Practitioners published the findings of a survey that showed that 70% of GPs contacted reported little or no support for their patients with dementia, or their families.

It puts me in mind of an article written by journalist Peter Hitchens, after the Conservative Party Conference. "How odd it would be to actually watch Oxford beat Cambridge by a mile in the Boat Race, and then open the papers next morning and read that Cambridge had won," he wrote. "Last week was a bit like that for me. I watched the Tory conference carefully. And then I read the papers, and it was all plain wrong." He went on to examine the way in which the implications of some of the propositions made, which the Party knew were not what people wanted, had been cloaked in mystery by the way in which they were presented. In other words, he unpicked the spin, which he called "terminological inexactitudes". What would he make of the push for early diagnosis, when ministers clearly know that medications help only one in three people, and that lack of care and support for those diagnosed leaves so many "adrift"?

Could it be, as I heard a speaker at a conference say, that there is a need to create a market to incentivize pharmaceutical companies at a time when they are cutting back on research and development because of the lack of success? Surely the Government would not push thousands of people into a diagnosis knowing that it would be sending them into a maze, blindfolded, which was how Jeremy Hughes, Chief Executive of the Alzheimer's Society, described it?[7]

Two-thirds of people with dementia are cared for in their own homes, by their families. The strain on family caregivers is enormous, often leading to physical and mental ill health which can continue for years after bereavement. "Tragedies are happening behind closed doors," said author Sir Terry Pratchett, when he took a personal interest after being diagnosed himself. Perhaps the deepest tragedies behind closed doors are for older people living entirely alone. Gloria Foster had been a larger-than-life character who loved music, animals, and playing bridge and golf. In her eighties she became a dementia sufferer, and received care in her own home from a registered agency, supervised by a council social worker. The agency was closed down by the UK Border Agency and the names of its clients passed to the council's Adult Social Services Department. The social worker assumed that, as Mrs Foster was paying for herself, she had made her own alternative arrangements, not considering, it seems, that an eighty-two-year-old with dementia might not have the capacity. Mrs Foster was left without care for nine days. When she was discovered by a district nurse she was lying in bed, soaked in urine and barely alive; in fact she died a day or so later in hospital. The coroner recorded a verdict of death by "natural causes contributed to by neglect". The journalist on the local press said that she could only feel pity for the social worker. "She cried as she gave evidence, and her career is ruined." Mrs Foster's brother-in-law said, "What lay behind it was the fact that the care services are under financial pressure. It seemed obvious from the evidence that was read that they [the county's social workers] were struggling to cope."

The family of seventy-year-old Elizabeth Anang did everything right after she'd been diagnosed with dementia. Her husband looked after her while he was alive, but after his death their daughter, Annemarie, turned to the local authority for help and advice; Mrs Anang appears to have been a "self-funder". The council recommended a care agency, who promised that Mrs Anang would be cared for on a daily basis, by a small team who would get to know her, and with whom she would become familiar. Instead, they sent thirty-five different carers in just six months. Some of them hadn't even been told that she had dementia, and most didn't know if she liked tea or coffee. Annemarie said, "The effect is terrible. Imagine being elderly and confused and so many different strangers coming and going and doing intimate things like washing you and feeding you. Most of the time you have no idea who they are because they've not had the time to build up any relationship with you. It's very distressing for someone with dementia to have to go through that sort of turnover."[8] Mrs Anang is now in a care home.

Professor John Ashton, president of the Faculty of Public Health, says that older people are being betrayed by a system that cannot afford to look after them. "They fought in World War Two or contributed to the war effort and wanted to create a secure environment that came to be known as the welfare state, which is now being portrayed as for dependants and layabouts. It is an abominable betrayal."

Here's hope

Brush aside the "terminological inexactitudes" and you see little glimpses of hope. Not from politicians or national charities, but from the determined people who are actually in the thick of it – the GPs, and other champions, like the Admiral Nurses, dementia champions, and individuals ignoring the rhetoric and taking positive action. Small but powerful little lights. They remind me of the man standing in "the square" in Paris with hundreds of others after a terrorist attack. He was lighting a candle. He told the interviewer, "We will not let the night fall on us. This candle is a small light. But even a small light is stronger than darkness. The darkness will not overwhelm us."

Rose George says that her city, Leeds, now has a great dementia-friendly strategy which is trying to improve matters in the teeth of huge financial cuts. "There are good initiatives, here and there. My mother has just been promised that there will be an Admiral Nurse in Wakefield, which is what she has been campaigning for since my dad died. This makes sense both morally and economically: a study by Norfolk NHS Trust found that an Admiral Nurse saved the Health Service £443,593 in a year, in reduced contact with GPs and nurses, and in the eight mental health bed referrals that were avoided. That's the kind of calculation that we should be making, not simply putting a bounty on diagnosis. More money would bring better training of staff such as that thoughtless junior doctor, the thoughtless GP, the thoughtless auxiliary who called a dementia patient 'a nasty man', when it's the disease that is nasty, not the person. Such endemic thoughtlessness shows that it's the system that's broken. It'll take more than £55 lollipops to fix it."

And it's good to know that we can put our faith in our first line of help, our family doctors. That they're not going to refer old people to Memory Clinics unless they are really sure that they showing clear symptoms. Despite pressure from the Government, it's heartening to know that our GPs want the best treatment for their patients. From articles in *Pulse* magazine and *The British Medical Journal* it's evident that many of them are knitting their eyebrows and thinking, like Peter Hitchens after the Tory Party conference, that "It's all plain wrong". That's very much a cause for hope, because it tells us that they won't let their patients be swept up in a political move, of whatever stripe. GPs such as Martin Brunet, who wrote to the press saying, "We need to stop the obsession with numbers... You wouldn't believe it from the headlines, but the prevalence of dementia is actually falling – that's half the undiagnosed cases dealt with... make me want to diagnose it by bringing real benefit to my patients. Isn't that what they deserve?"

Dr Brunet has come up with a plan that is simple, and affordable. He suggests a Memory Worker attached to every GP practice, someone who will visit the patient's home within days of a diagnosis. He said, "They don't need to be nurses but they need to have time: time to listen; time to sit; time to visit regularly so that they become a familiar face, a friend even; a travelling companion on the journey called dementia." Thousands of Memory Workers are needed, even if each one covered two or three practices.[9]

The scheme could be funded by diverting "wasted money" tied up in the hospital dementia Commissioning for Quality and Innovation (CQIN) payment. This is a payment to hospital trusts to identify elderly patients admitted to hospital with undiagnosed dementia; in reality, says Dr Brunet, the CQIN payment is an expensive box-ticking exercise of questionable value. "A Trust can earn around £1 million per year from the CQIN, and with 160 trusts in England that would boost the pot substantially." With the money diverted to tailored care and support, it could even help patients with dementia avoid hospital admission.

Barriers to diagnosis could be reduced by bringing the Memory Clinic doctor to patients' familiar practices, instead of expecting them to find their way around intimidating corridors in unfamiliar hospitals. It would also mean that no one need feel as cut adrift as seventy-three-year-old Shelagh Robinson, who spent less than five minutes with the Memory Clinic doctor. Her brain scans had shown she had dementia and was suitable for medication. She said, "They said they would write to my GP, arrange the necessary tests, and see me in twelve weeks. It was like being told I had tonsillitis. That afternoon was one of the worst of my life because of the total lack of empathy and support. I didn't know where to turn." The Memory Workers would be able to support people like Shelagh as well as family members. There need be no more cases like Mrs Foster's, because the Memory Worker wouldn't forget her even if the social worker did.

* * *

At the crossroads

"It's all down to money," said a psychiatrist when I asked about the lack of real care for family caregivers. It seems unlikely that hospital trusts would relinquish a revenue stream at a time when they are hard-pressed for cash and coping with increasing demand, and budgets for social care are predicted to be squashed even tighter for the next few years. There are more and more allusions to the cost of caring for an elderly population, and, although we may not have realized it, we are at a major crossroads. The road we're on is potholed with ageism, indifference, deflection, and terminological inexactitudes. We can continue on it, hoping that somewhere, someone will come up with the solution. Or we could find ourselves being persuaded to take the same road as Belgium and the Netherlands, and Oregon in the USA, where euthanasia in the form of assisted suicide, euphemistically labelled "dying with dignity" has become law.

Among those euthanized in Holland in 2013 were ninety-seven people with dementia and a woman in her eighties who didn't want to live in a care home. The figures didn't include cases of so-called "terminal sedation", where patients are given a cocktail of sedatives and narcotics before food and fluids are withdrawn. Studies suggest that if such deaths were added to the figure then euthanasia would account for one in eight – about 12.3 per cent – of all deaths in the Netherlands. In 2014, Dutch Regulator Professor Boer, who has reviewed 4,000 cases of euthanasia in his role as a regulator, advised the British Parliament not to adopt it. Once a firm advocate of euthanasia, he said that he realized now that the Dutch had been "terribly wrong" to think they could control it. He said his country has witnessed an "explosive increase" in the numbers of euthanasia deaths since 2007 and that he expected the number of such deaths in 2014 to hit 6,000. He was also gravely concerned by the extension of euthanasia to new classes of people, including those with dementia and the depressed. "Some slopes truly are slippery," he said. There were reports of older people in Holland carrying "I do not want to be euthanized" cards in their wallets. In one of the most shocking cases, a man described how he arranged the double euthanasia of his parents, in their eighties, who wanted to die because they were afraid of loneliness – how many searching questions does this provoke?

Former government minister Lord Tebbit, whose wife was left paralysed by the IRA bombing in Brighton in 1984, said that legalizing euthanasia "would provide a route to great pressure on the elderly, the sick and the disabled to do the decent thing and cease to be a burden on others. Those who care for such people are all too familiar with the moments of black despair that prompt those words, 'I would be better dead, so that you could get on with your life'. This Bill will be a breeding ground for vultures, individual and corporate. It creates too much financial incentive for the taking of life." Lively-minded vicar Michael Wenham who was diagnosed with Primary Lateral Sclerosis, a type of motor neurone disease, in 2002 foresees a possibility that, when a diagnosis like his is given in the future, if euthanasia were legal, assisted suicide could be offered as an optional "treatment", although he profoundly doubts that many doctors would want to suggest it. The danger then would be that if the suicide option were refused, the elderly and disabled would feel that they were draining the country's resources. The financial cost of caring for the elderly has been flagged many times. An example is former Member of Parliament Chris Huhne, who wrote, "Someone needs to fight the selfish, short-sighted old," adding that "the cost of pandering to pensioners means we are penalising our young in relation to education, healthcare and housing".[10]

A major cause of the crisis in NHS hospitals last winter was portrayed in the media as elderly people clogging up A&E (Accident and Emergency) units and taking up hospital beds. There seemed to be at least one new story with this slant every week. Then a report by Quality Watch, an initiative of the Health Foundation and Nuffield Trust think tanks, revealed that the heaviest users of A&E were people in their twenties. Twenty per cent of A&E attendances are alcohol-related, a figure that rises to 80 per cent during peak weekend periods on Friday and Saturday nights. Each year, more than one million hospital admissions in England are alcohol-related. Over the last decade, such admissions in those aged between fifteen and twenty-nine have risen by almost 60 per cent. But this report, carefully written by leading journalist Andrew Gilligan,[11] was not taken up and reported widely by the BBC or other outlets.

Another hope we have "going forward" (I'm not sure if I like that expression or not, but it says what I mean here), is that while older people are generally not very good at speaking up for themselves, if the upcoming Baby Boomers (those born in the 1950s) live up to their reputation, they will not take neglect and "inexactitudes" quietly. But the Bible says that we are to expose things that are not right (Ephesians 5:11) and to speak up for the disadvantaged: "Speak up for those who cannot speak for themselves, for the rights of all who are destitute. Speak up and judge fairly; defend the rights of the poor and needy" (Proverbs 31:8, 9, NIV). Christian organizations such as The Christian

Institute and Christian Concern are constantly fighting on a whole range of issues, but we shouldn't leave it all to them.

The evangelical movements of the 1800s are a testament to the power of ordinary Christians to bring change. Their work provoked social changes that helped Britain avoid the bloody revolutions that took place in other countries. Among them were people like Charles Spurgeon, the great preacher, the Earl of Shaftesbury, the determined reformer, and William Wilberforce, the passionate anti-slavery campaigner. In fact, Wilberforce became vice-president of the Aged Pilgrims' Friend Society until his death in 1835, convinced as he was of the value of each soul to God, and this little charity's dogged persistence in the face of apathy and indifference brought about changes in care for the elderly that still exist today.

In 1807 conditions in Great Britain were unbelievably dire. The Napoleonic Wars had depleted the economy, and there were bread riots. The Land Enclosure Bills which rippled over the country from 1604 until 1914 took just over 6.8 million acres of strips of common land that had been farmed by yeoman and tenant farmers and consolidated them into individually owned or rented fields, removing their livelihood. There was a mass exodus into the towns from the country, as people looked for work. Our old books show older people living in garrets and sleeping on straw. There were widows who were left destitute when their husbands died, because there was no welfare state in those days. The Aged Pilgrims' Friend Society helped them with regular pensions and practical goods. On record is a letter accompanying a parcel of groceries with instructions on how to open the enclosed tin of treacle, which was said to be good for warding off winter ailments. (It was to be opened by punching a hole in the top!)

Now we are facing a different kind of indifference to older people. A widow in her eighties with dementia died because her social worker made a mistake. Another was subjected to care from dozens of people termed "carers" who didn't care whether she liked tea or coffee. Councils tighten eligibility rules so extremely that many lonely, frail people can't obtain care at all, and are facing "catastrophe". Care homes are paid less than half the cost of the care in some areas. Thousands of home carers (domiciliary carers) are paid less than the legal minimum wage because their wages don't include travel time and costs of travel between homes. There have been protests since 2011, but still nothing has been changed. These are only the tip of the iceberg.

Under the surface, out of sight, terrible things are happening to some. Last year an estimated 14,000 people aged over seventy-five were denied cancer treatment by "ageist" consultants, according to a report by the charity Macmillan Cancer Support.[12] And while Age UK found that 900,000 were facing catastrophe because they couldn't obtain funding for care, tens of thousands had been unlawfully removed from their homes and detained against their will in locked care homes and EMI (Elderly Mentally Infirm) hospital wards. In many cases their assets, including their homes, had been seized by councils to pay for their care. You may want to read that again, because it sounds too outrageous to be true, but it is.

After a long investigation into the workings of the Mental Capacity Act, which includes the Deprivation of Liberty Safeguards, the Lords' Scrutiny Committee reported to

Parliament. The report and an easy-to-read account of the investigation are on these websites:

- http://www.publications.parliament.uk/pa/ld201314/ ldselect/ldmentalcap/139/139.pdf

- http://www.parliament.uk/business/committees/ committees-a-z/lords-select/mental-capacity-act-2005/ news/mca-press-release---13-march-2014/

Journalist Christopher Booker has been campaigning against the secrecy of the Court of Protection and the Family Courts for some years, and had been following several stories of injustices to older people, which he had been banned by law from publishing. He wrote, "While the Lords' report is savagely critical of how this system works, finding that it is too often used to detain old people illegally, it scarcely touches on the terrifying consequences of this incarceration for elderly and vulnerable individuals up and down Britain."[13]

He describes some heartbreaking cases, including that of a husband forbidden to see his wife ever again after reporting the poor care she was getting at the home she'd been forcibly taken to; he was even forbidden to send her flowers or Christmas and birthday cards. He is heartbroken and has had no contact with her for years.

A few months after the report to Parliament, Sir James Munby, President of the Family Division of the High Court, said it was clear that the number of people forcibly deprived of their liberty on mental health grounds had been "vastly" underestimated, and that there would be an avalanche of legal challenges so great that he doubted that the Court of Protection would be able to cope. "Councils could also face an "immense burden" from the cost of the extra legal cases, he warned. "I want to try to bring some measure of administrative order and proper process into play in the light of the ramifications of the recent judgment of the Supreme Court."[14]

The first of the cases surfaced in February 2015, with an excoriating ruling by Judge Paul Mort against the council concerned. He said, "A defenceless 91-year-old gentleman in the final years of his life was removed from his home of 50 years and detained in a locked dementia unit against his wishes. Had it not been for the alarm raised by his friend he may have been condemned to remain there for the remainder of his days." He ruled that the ninety-one-year-old must immediately be released to go home, where he could be properly looked after, and the council must pay all his care and legal costs, plus hefty damages. The ruling can be seen on the BAILII website (http://www.bailii.org/) under (2015) EWCOP 1. Sadly, another man, an eighty-year-old, had no one to speak up for him, and his only son was living abroad at the time. A neighbour had complained to the council that he was being neglected, and social workers took him into care. The council began to sell his house, including valuable family heirlooms (to the neighbour who had complained), to pay for his care and mounting legal costs. His son, who returned when he heard, was only allowed limited care home visits, which were eventually stopped altogether. On three separate occasions the eighty-year-old was attacked with a stick by another resident "in care" and lost seven of his teeth. He eventually died of pneumonia.

Older people seem to have become political pawns and

scapegoats, and if we ignore the situation we are not only letting them down but are laying up a very uncertain future for ourselves. We can pressure politicians, and we can be praying for them, too. Decisions made in Government affect every one of us, and we can be encouraged by what the Bible says in Proverbs 21:1 (NASB): "The king's heart is like channels of water in the hand of the Lord; He turns it wherever He wishes." We can ask Him to take the hearts of those who make decisions that affect the vulnerable and turn them towards godly decisions. After all, we believers are linked to the Creator of the Universe, Someone who has the power to hold the world in His hand and to stop the sun going down for a whole day (Joshua 10:13).

There are signs that the Christian church, which has stepped into the gap in times of great need in the past, is stirring again. A pastoral team drove for three hours to a national conference just to hear our talk on "Empowering Older People". That's all they wanted. They made notes and talked to us for over an hour afterwards. More and more churches are actively supporting older people, including those with dementia and their families, and we're continually hearing from pastoral teams and church leaders who are rolling out a whole range of projects. These are great pathways to hope.

Notes

1. John Bingham, Social Affairs Editor, *The Daily Telegraph*, 2 July 2014.
2. http://www.bmj.com/content/345/bmj.e8588?ijkey=d9TRTbB8ZT4ym82&keytype=ref
3. http://www.theguardian.com/commentisfree/2014/oct/28/solve-dementia-crisis-paying-gps
4. http://www.alzheimers.org.uk/site/scripts/news_article.php?newsID=2077
5. http://www.telegraph.co.uk/health/nhs/11088603/Jeremy-Hunt-NHS-must-stop-giving-dementia-patients-short-straw.html

6. http://www.pulsetoday.co.uk/clinical/therapy-areas/neurology/hunt-vows-to-change-gps-minds-over-dementia-diagnosis/20002630.article#.VMI_TP6sVyw

7. http://www.independent.co.uk/life-style/health-and-families/health-news/dementia-sufferers-are-cut-adrift-after-diagnosis-warning-9577326.html

8. http://www.telegraph.co.uk/health/elderhealth/11305679/Dozens-of-carers-in-two-months-but-no-one-knew-whether-mum-liked-tea-or-coffee.html

9. http://www.telegraph.co.uk/health/healthnews/11222003/Dementia-I-dont-want-a-55-bribe-to-diagnose-patients.html

10. http://www.theguardian.com/commentisfree/2013/dec/22/someone-needs-fight-selfish-old

11. http://www.telegraph.co.uk/health/nhs/11337654/Put-up-drink-prices-to-stop-AandE-crisis-say-doctors.html; http://www.telegraph.co.uk/health/nhs/11337430/Why-this-AandE-crisis-isnt-a-simple-emergency-about-cash.html

12. http://www.macmillan.org.uk/Documents/GetInvolved/Campaigns/AgeOldExcuse/AgeOldExcuseReport-MacmillanCancerSupport.pdf

13. http://www.dailymail.co.uk/news/article-2580636/Read-stories-secret-courts-imprison-elderly-care-homes-against-weep.html#ixzz3TRbyHEf9

14. http://www.telegraph.co.uk/news/health/news/10818296/Courts-braced-for-surge-in-cases-of-elderly-locked-up-against-their-will.html

Chapter 5
Strength for the Journey

How preparing for old age strengthens us even through the dementia journey

> *If you have run with footmen and they have tired you out,*
> *Then how can you compete with horses?*
> *If you fall down in a land of peace,*
> *How will you do in the thicket of the Jordan?*
> *(Jeremiah 12:5, NASB)*

It's going to get tougher, not easier, God is telling Jeremiah. There's a widely held assumption that people who've been Christians for a long time will find their spiritual and emotional life easier as they grow older; that having been through the deep waters and fiery trials and proved God's faithfulness, they will sail serenely through old age. If only! Famous English evangelist John Stott said, "I knew I had to prepare for eternity, but no one told me I had to prepare for being old." International preacher Billy Graham said, "All my life I was taught how to die as a Christian, but no one ever taught me how I ought to live in the years before I die… It is not easy." And Jeff Lucas, author and teaching pastor of the large Timberline Church in Colorado, wrote, "Nobody told me anything about the one thing you never believe will happen when you're young but happens to every human on the planet. And that is that we will all grow old."

How is it that we can see the challenges that old age brings to others but fail to anticipate them for ourselves? Perhaps it's because we're able to relate to others at every stage of life that we ourselves have experienced, but not old age, because we haven't – yet. "Preparing for a Great Old Age" is one of our seminars that has people's heads nodding and eyes widening as they see things in sharp focus for the first time. Encouragingly, many in the audience are pastoral team workers who want older people in their churches to be empowered.

Something else to bear in mind is that the enemy of our souls, who prowls around looking for souls to devour (1 Peter 5:8), seems especially to like older saints whose souls have been tenderized by the Holy Spirit. Living in old age is not easy. It's not a place for sissies, as formidable actress Bette Davis once said. Neither is living with dementia, which has been described as "the scourge of old age", and is predicted to have an impact on the lives of one in three of us, in one way or another. The preparation we make for old age will also take us safely through the dementia journey.

The key is in Proverbs 4:23: "Above everything else, guard your heart; for it is the source of life's consequences" (CJB). It is so important that it can literally mean life or death for people caring for loved ones with dementia. They're known to researchers and social workers as "caregivers", but they don't see themselves that way. They are really the husbands, wives, sons and daughters, brothers and sisters and close friends who find themselves thrust into this unexpected, life-critical role, usually with no education or training.

Horatio Spafford's lovely 1873 hymn has the chorus, "It is well, it is well, with my soul", and states that even when sorrows like sea billows roll, the singer has peace in the soul. There can be few storms as fierce as the dementia journey, and we've met only a handful of people who said that they had peace in their soul the whole time. Many have emotional scars that continue to affect them, sometimes years after the bereavement.

"I'm still angry," said a daughter, seven years after the death of her mother. "I'm angry at the whole thing."

A former social worker felt the same, three years after her husband's death. "So angry!" she said. "I should have been given more information, and offered counselling. No one should have to go through years of this without that kind of support." A parish worker found that, years after her mother had died, she could still find herself overtaken by grief. Grief, anger, and guilt are strong emotions that can leave lasting scars on the dementia caregiver's soul.

The health of close family members caring for a loved one with dementia can be so badly affected by negative emotions that they are sometimes referred to as the "hidden victims".[1] The syndrome is known as "dementia caregiver burden", and the transference to their bodies has been observed in poorer immune responses to viral challenges, slower rates of wound healing, and significantly higher levels of plasma insulin than age-matched control subjects. They are at a higher risk than non-caregiving age-matched controls for developing mild hypertension and have an increased tendency to develop a serious illness as well as increased risk for all-cause mortality, including greater cardiovascular risks. They are also more at risk of developing dementia themselves: the high prevalence of depression in dementia caregivers has been well documented and depression is known to increase the risk of dementia.

A couple living in our housing scheme came in for care and support when the wife developed dementia, but now, after about five years of caring, the devoted husband is developing it himself, too.

If you have read *Dementia: Frank and Linda's Story*, you will have seen how Linda's rheumatoid arthritis grew much worse towards the end of their journey. Newly retired James coped with his wife's dementia with stoicism and a strong managing style: "I say to the Lord, right, whatever you send me, I'll cope with it, a day at a time." When he first retired, he said, he felt so full of energy that he didn't know what to do with himself. After a few years as a caregiver he developed a cardiovascular condition and needed an operation to insert stents to open his arteries. In fact, dementia caregiver burden can be so damaging that, as mentioned earlier, it is not uncommon for elderly spouses to die before their loved one. The objective part, the practical acts of daily living, the washing, the feeding, even being the Atlas holding everything together, do not cause caregiver burden. It's the emotional roller coaster, the grief of continuing loss, the loss of the relationship with the person – the personality – you used to know, the hope of the future, and the stress, the anxiety and hypervigilance, the feelings of guilt and inadequacy, and so on: these are what batter the soul.

Clearing out unwanted baggage

The importance of recognizing negative emotions and their detrimental effect on health was recognized by brain scientist Jill Bolte Taylor, on her journey of recovery after suffering a massive brain haemorrhage. She discovered that, as parts of her brain's left hemisphere came back to life, "old files" were opened, and some of her negative emotional baggage surfaced. As only a neuroscientist could put it, she wrote that she needed to "evaluate the usefulness of preserving its underlying neural circuit". In other words, unhelpful baggage was not to have a place in her brain, it was not wanted on the rest of her journey. Understanding how her neural circuitry worked, she declared that, "No one had the power to make me feel anything except for me and my brain." And she asserted that, although she was not going to be in total control of what happened to her in her life, "I am certainly in charge of how I choose to perceive my experience." "I made the cognitive choice to stay out of my own way during the process of recovery," she wrote, "being very careful about my self-talk."[2]

Jill's experience changed her life, not just because she was a neuroscientist and acutely conscious of how her brain worked, but because she was *aware* of what was happening and consciously chose to discard negative emotions. She identified the neural circuits that keep them alive and chose to deactivate them, overlaying them instead with positive thoughts and feelings, such as joy and gratitude at being alive. She may not have known it, but she was applying Philippians 4:8, and focusing her thoughts on "what is true, noble, righteous, pure, lovable or admirable, on some virtue or on something praiseworthy" (CJB). A similar approach is taken by Christian author Dr Caroline Leaf, in her book that describes the pathology of thinking and our choices, *Who Switched Off My Brain?*[3]

Jill's knowledge of the brain and her determination to recover enforced almost a hyper self-awareness, but the case is almost the opposite with dementia caregivers. Most are so busy simply getting through the day and doing their best for their loved one that, as a rule, they have no idea of the emotional toll it is taking on them. They tend to take very little care of themselves. And because dementia caregiving can be isolating and lonely, they're often unaware that others are affected in the same way. This includes even counsellors and psychotherapists who are used to recognizing dysfunctional perceptions and their emotional impacts.

A couple of years ago I presented a synopsis of my research at a conference at my university. During the question time at the end, there were a few polite questions, and a lady in the front row who had been a caregiver herself said, "You must write a book about this." At the close, as we all walked back to the coffee bar, another of the participants came alongside and said, "Thank you for that. My mother has dementia, and I'm her main carer. I had no idea that other people felt the way I do. That is quite a relief to me." Then, at the coffee counter in the line inching forward slowly, another man turned to me and said, "Seeing everything laid out in your presentation, it makes so much sense. I hadn't seen it like that before." He was caring for his father. They were experienced counsellors.

At a conference day on dementia, in a seminar about caregivers looking after themselves, I explained, among other things, a little about complicated grief. Grief is part of life; everyone experiences it at some time. Even Jesus was a "man of sorrows and acquainted with grief" (Isaiah 53:3). But complicated grief is different. It's grieving that's mixed with other emotions – a sense of injustice and inadequacy, anger, and guilt as well as sadness. This mixture makes it difficult to resolve, and complicated grief can feel so intense that it overwhelms bereaved caregivers. They may ruminate obsessively about things that happened before the death and blame themselves or others for it. There may have been a long period of grieving over losses before the actual death, yet no one seemed to have noticed, or empathized. Grief becomes "disenfranchised". At the end of the day everyone left the hall to walk to the church hall across the road for a final service. I was still at the back, stuffing my laptop into my briefcase before following them, when I saw a lady in her fifties, with a very thoughtful expression, leave the others and come back to where I was standing. She said, in a wobbly voice, "What you said about complicated grief – I hadn't heard that before. But now I recognize it. I realize I've been suffering with it for years. It's taken over my life. It's affected my daughter, and my husband. My daughter says she's lost her mum, because I've changed."

Elaine's mother had been living near Elaine's older sister and her husband in another part of the country when she'd been diagnosed with dementia. The sister and husband decided that it would be better for their mother to move to a care home near Elaine because they didn't have time to look after her. Elaine felt worried and dismayed, because she and her mother had not had a particularly close relationship, but, nevertheless, she did her best. Spending time with her mother and managing her care deflected a measure of energy and time from her own family. But she thought she had no choice; she *ought* to do it.

It rankled that the responsibility had been dropped onto her, especially when the sister gave advice, usually critical, from a distance. She struggled for years with resentment, inadequacy, stress, depression, guilt, loss, and grief. She felt she'd become a bad mother, because it meant she spent so much time away from her family. Guilt can be a particular burden for Christians, because we feel we ought not to feel resentment; that we ought not to harbour these feelings, and we should be a better person: that, in fact, it's our entire fault. We have so many "oughts" and "shoulds". Would preachers please point out that the standards we aim for are there to draw us on, not to condemn us? We'll never attain them this side of glory, but so many Christians don't seem to realize this.

The principle in John 8:32, which says "you shall see the truth and the truth shall set you free," holds true in any context. We looked together at the threads running through the "garment of heaviness" that had weighed her down for so long. She was glad to untangle them, forgive the relatives, acknowledge the grief, and begin to let it go. Looking back over her years of caring, she saw that she'd actually done a good job. Her own family were settled, and they enjoyed each other's company. We sat for a long time, talking and praying, and thanking God. There was still some work for her to do, but the sense of release was palpable.

Some caregivers cope better than others. Researchers note a number of reasons for this. Having a strong sense of coherence (SOC) is one. A person's sense of coherence refers to their enduring feeling of confidence and ability to cope with whatever happens in life and that life's demands are worthy of investment and engagement.[4] People with a strong SOC tend to build emotional resilience, and a positive attitude. They're a bit like those Weebles™, rounded at the bottom so that, however hard you try to push them over, they'll spring up again.

Knowing the spiritual resources that God gives us daily, through the Holy Spirit who lives in us and guides us, wouldn't you think that we would all be the Arnold Schwarzeneggers of SOC? That it would be so strong in us that all negative emotions and distorted thinking would bounce off our spiritual muscles? That we would stride into dementia and knock its socks off! But none of us is complete in Christ yet. We're still a work in progress, and Christ is still being formed in us (Galatians 4:19).

So what do we need to do, to be ready to run with horsemen? (Jeremiah 12:5)

If we are running a race, we need to be sure that nothing trips us up. It's as true in the spiritual sense as in the physical. The psalmist David understood this principle when he asked the Lord, in Psalm 139, "Search me, O God, and know my heart: try me, and know my thoughts: and see if there be any wicked way in me, and lead me in the way everlasting (KJV)." It is amazing to think that God knows us better than we know ourselves. Most of us have hidden tripwires – they are the automatic negative thoughts that zip through our minds. Have you ever seen one of the old steam trains go under a bridge? If they hooted, the steam they left behind would stay around long after the train had gone. Negative thoughts are like that. They zip through but leave a stifling cloud.

David was particularly insightful, as most of us don't even begin to think about our inner selves. We just get on with lives, coping as best we can. People come to counselling only when they've hit a psychological barrier, or their relationships aren't working. The lady whose bare face, without make-up, had only ever been seen by her husband and her surgeon, had no idea why she felt defective without cosmetics. She just knew that she did. The businessman who lost contracts, despite his talents, because he felt disagreements were a rejection of him personally: the father whose family nicknamed him "Basil" after the character in the 1970s BBC TV comedy *Fawlty Towers* because of his quick, explosive anger; the mother who couldn't engage with her own babies – these were all Christians reacting to deeply hidden negative schemas. A schema is a set of core beliefs about ourselves, other people, and the world. They begin to be formed from the moment we are born, and are such an intrinsic part of us that we are as unaware of them as we are of the corpuscles that course through our blood. All our automatic assumptions spring from this schema. We may believe that we are likeable, and capable, and other people are likeable and can be trusted, and the world is more or less OK. Or we may believe that we are not likeable, and so on. Bullying in school years has a terribly detrimental, long-lasting effect, leading us to believe even as adults that people will reject us. They produce an instant default position in any situation.

Calvin, in his 1536 work *Institutes of the Christian Religion*, says that we cannot truly understand God until we understand ourselves. Calvin may have been thinking of our sinful nature, but, nevertheless, what he said is true.

Jill Bolte Taylor's knowledge of how her brain worked helped in her self-discovery. She was able to link her feelings with her thoughts and the underlying brain structure in an extraordinarily analytical way. Most of us rarely approach that level of analysis and self-awareness. But, like Jill, we want to be fully functioning, emotionally, mentally, and spiritually fit human beings. Ready for anything life throws at us, including dementia or being a caregiver. Something else we share with Jill is that we're not aware of our negative thoughts until we experience a crisis.

In cognitive behavioural therapy there's a process called "case conceptualization". It's collaboration between the counsellor and the person being counselled. It's a journey of self-discovery going top-down, from the issue being presented (which could be a fear of not being accepted by the work team), to the root cause, which could be, say, bullying in school, which is quite common. The effects can last for a lifetime. There are techniques that can help the person deal with it at this primary level, as well as in the here and now. It nearly always involves forgiveness.

This was very hard for Sheryl, whose mother used her as a punch bag, literally, for most of her childhood. It happened only when her father was away working. Terrified of her mother, Sheryl summoned up the courage to tell her father, just once, what was happening. He had no idea of the viciousness of the beatings and remonstrated with his wife mildly, but afterwards her mother told Sheryl that if she ever spoke to him again about it, she would kill her. Sheryl felt trapped, and decided that the only way to cope was to shut down her feelings. She was eight years old. She remembers forming the decision sitting on a tree swing at the bottom of the garden. From that moment on she suppressed all her emotions; she would simply choose to feel nothing. (Notice that Jill did not *suppress* negative emotions;

79

she dismissed them altogether and chose alternatives.) When I met Sheryl she was a highly regarded medical professional, looking for respect not affection, for affirmation of worth from achievement, not for who she was herself.

Her undoing was meeting a man who loved her for herself, a big bear of a man with unconditional love. Her ice walls began to melt and tides of suppressed emotions threatened to overwhelm her. There were many knots to undo and threads to unpick, but it came to the point at which the entire edifice of Sheryl's emotional health pivoted on one single factor – she had to forgive her mother. What made it harder was that the nearest her mother ever got to acknowledging her cruelty was to say that she'd spent years suffering from premenstrual tension. She was now a pillar of her local church and a model of rectitude. It was very hard for Sheryl, but she found release through a kind of practical pathway to forgiveness, outlined by Christian psychologist Norman H. Wright in his book *Making Peace with Your Past*. It may be out of print now, but some second-hand book retailers may have it, and I recommend it for your bookshelf. Forgiveness is essential, but it's not always easy.

There are other helpful books. There is a particularly good one by Greenberger and Padesky, called *Mind over Mood*, and there are other books on the market, including *CBT for Dummies*. There's also one by a hospital doctor who was able to give up years of smoking after seeing how CBT "worked" for drug addicts, entitled *Stop Smoking with CBT*.[5] (A list of recommended books is in Appendix 2.)

Jill Bolte Taylor wrote that, "as a society, we do not teach our children that they need to tend carefully the garden of their minds."[6] She said, too, that "none of us came into the world with a manual about how to get it right".[7] But everything we need is right there in the Bible. A teacher friend was telling me how children in her primary school are being taught values. She said, "They include things like – being kind to one another, respecting others, helping others, being truthful … they're ALL Christian values, they're all there in the Bible." Then she added, "But, of course, you can't actually say that!"

Time and time again it strikes me how much more we are enabled to live, in every aspect, in Christ. He really is as He says He is – the way, the truth, and the life. We can get to know ourselves by absorbing the Scriptures and doing what they say, and being continually filled with the Holy Spirit (Ephesians 5:18.) The Scriptures are bedrock truth, and the Holy Spirit reveals things to us and moulds us. He is constantly helping us to renew the spirit of our minds (Ephesians 4:23).

Jesus described it as like building a house on rock. It makes such sense. He said:

> *Everyone then who hears these words of mine and does them will be like a wise man who built his house on the rock. And the rain fell, and the floods came, and the winds blew and beat on that house, but it did not fall, because it had been founded on the rock. And everyone who hears these words of mine and does not do them will be like a foolish man who built his house on the sand. And the rain fell, and the floods came, and the winds blew and beat against that house, and it fell, and great was the fall of it. (Matthew 7:24–27, ESV)*

We *hear* it, we *do* it, and it changes us. In CBT terms, it's referred to as building healthy schemas, those core beliefs that are like tectonic plates on which our personality rests; sound spiritual schemas that will protect our minds and our hearts like the armour described in Ephesians 6. The reason the CBT approach works, I believe, is that it's simply scriptural truth presented in a different framework. It's helped thousands of people and seems to have become the "talking therapy" of choice for the NHS. But, as a good friend said, "Salt is salt whatever it's called – it does the same thing."

A schema becomes our individual mind map through which we instantly interpret everything in our world. It is our subliminal "blink" reference.[8] It's not a programme of personal development; it's about becoming like Jesus and being "conformed to His image" (Romans 8:29). It's about having such a close relationship with Him that we become like Him, so when our lives are lashed by storms we can be as calm as He was on that stormy night in the boat on the lake of Galilee.

Someone said to me that our highly individual schemas are "like having a vegetable colander on your head. You only see through the holes right in front of your eyes". Getting people with faulty schemas to adjust their "vegetable colander" so that they can see a fuller picture is one of the aims of cognitive behavioural therapy. I think it's one of the aims of the Scriptures, too! Sadly, there are many who are convinced they are only of value when they are striving to achieve worthy goals, or have reached them, because that's what they learned from their early-years environment. They felt that they were not valued for themselves, only for their accomplishments. Some become high achievers, but even when they are successful they can be left with an "impostor syndrome", feeling that if people really knew them they would see that they are a fraud.

Sometimes there are exacting parents who do not value even the child's achievement. These children, when they become adults, are left with a permanent sense of disappointment and a "What's the point?" attitude. Whatever they did never made the grade for Mum or Dad. Brian lived for most of his life with low-grade depression and would actually say, "What's the point?" quite frequently. He remembered getting B grades (next to top A grade) in school and his father saying, "Only a B! With a bit more work you could have got an A!" and many similar instances. When he was a child his parents never affirmed his achievements, or his worth. So one of his core beliefs as an adult was that nothing he did would make a difference. It was a psychological handicap all his life. He knew he was talented enough in his career to apply for promotion, but he would tell himself, "What's the point?"

The importance of negative schemas is that they lead to negative or dysfunctional thinking. For example, if Brian ever found himself caring for his wife with dementia his negative thinking would tell him that nothing he did would make a difference, and that he was a poor caregiver. He would know it for sure; it would be an automatic negative thought running through his subconscious every waking moment. Brian would probably begin to blame himself for the inevitable deterioration in her condition, thinking it would be his fault because he wasn't up to it. A bit like the lady whose brother told her she was always slow in catching up.

The late American psychologist Susan Jeffers is best remembered for her 1987 book *Feel the Fear and Do it Anyway*. When you feel you are not capable of doing something, she says you should say to yourself, "I can do anything! I can do anything!" until you believe it. But we have something much more powerful to change our thinking. We can say to ourselves, "I can do all things through him who strengthens me" (Philippians 4:13, ESV). These are not just any old words. "For the word of God is alive and active. Sharper than any double-edged sword, it penetrates even to dividing soul and spirit, joints and marrow; it judges the thoughts and attitudes of the heart." When you feel you're not up to it, that it's going to be tough, write that scripture on a Post-it™ note and stick it up where you'll see it several times a day. Repeat it to yourself. Put it on your phone or tablet so it will spring up and catch your eye.

When we build in ourselves a cognitive template that becomes our instinctive way of thinking, we are allowing the Holy Spirit to work in us and change the way we think and the way we feel about ourselves. It also changes the way we talk to ourselves. We chatter to ourselves in our minds more or less continually from the minute we wake to the minute we go to sleep. Some of the chatter is so fast and deep we don't notice it, but it affects how we feel. Our Christian discipline is to align our thinking with scriptural truths.

It's a real hope. We see it realized in some of the older people in our "bundle of the living" (1 Samuel 25:29). People such as Dorothy (name changed), the eighty-two-year-old who stayed on in our care home for ten years after her husband's death to minister to others, when she could have gone back to her comfortable apartment. Each morning her room was like a cathedral, she told me, as she spent time with the Lord praying for each person in the home. Staff loved her, and after she died the manager said it was "as if a light had gone out" in the home. A former nurse, Dorothy had cared for over thirty years for her husband, who had a degenerative disease, until her strength gave out. She'd agonized over her only daughter, who turned to a sect instead of having proper treatment for breast cancer, rejecting her faith and her mother in the process. Dorothy's anguished response was, "What shall I do, Lord? How can I pray?" The answer was, "Deliver her from evil," so that was Dorothy's prayer. And He did: there was a blessed reconciliation and she recommitted her life to Jesus shortly before she died. In all the events in her life, good and bad, Dorothy's default position sprang from a lifelong relationship with Jesus Christ.

We need to understand, too, that old age is not a mistake: it's actually part of God's plan for humanity. Older people are meant to cascade wisdom and the joy of the Lord, gleaned from a lifetime's experience of living with Him. They have a special purpose, part of which is to be like "lamps set on a hill", to tell out all that He has done (Psalm 105:1–5; Psalm 78:1–4).

Enjoying a great old age is the theme of my next book, but I began this chapter by quoting two famous Christians who said they hadn't been prepared for it, so I'll end by saying that the best way of preparing for old age is to become involved with older people and get to know them well. It may be that one of the reasons Dorothy was "great" in her old age was that, as a nurse, she had learned about it from her experience with frail old folk.

Old age nowadays isn't what it used to be! "Sixty is young," said a newspaper headline, and, according to the people we speak to at conference, seventy isn't bad either! Many people are living longer, with excellent health. I was asked to speak about befriending older people by a man who wanted to recruit supporters for the care home he and his wife had moved to, because she had dementia. David wanted the ethos of the home (not one of ours) to be more strongly Christian, and emailed local churches, inviting them to come to the "Launch of Bethel Friends" meeting, and arranged the whole thing. After the event he wrote a piece for the local press, which was published, word for word, unedited. David is ninety-three years old.

So we are thinking of frailer older people in their late eighties, nineties, and even hundreds. Try to experience old age through their eyes. A psychiatrist friend said that the four-letter word that sums up old age is LOSS. The roles that so defined us in life and gave us a strong sense of purpose and identity are gone. We grow more frail and lose strength, and we're not free to do things spontaneously, like pop into the car and visit friends, as we used to. (Old bladders usually need lots of loo stops.) We lose people we love and trust as they go Home ahead of us and, without their natural affirmation, can begin to lose faith in our own judgment. We may have spent our lives working with and enjoying others, but now we have to learn to live more internally, enjoying ourselves and the Lord. Also, remember, the "enemy of our souls" sees an easy target.

Essentially, the pathway to a good old age and coping with dementia is the same. It means taking care of your emotional, mental, and spiritual life. It also means taking care of your body! More and more research is showing that exercise does quite amazing things. It reverses brain shrinkage (often the cause of grumpiness in older men), regrows brain cells, stimulates healthy neurones, diminishes if not banishes depression, and delays the onset of cardiovascular disease and dementia. It cuts the risk of breast cancer by 25 per cent and bowel cancer by 34 per cent. A thirty-five-year study of 2,500 people in Caerphilly, in Wales, found that exercise, combined with a good diet, delayed heart disease by twelve years and dementia by sixteen years. A report by a leading surgeon for the Academy of Medical Royal Colleges called it a "Miracle Cure", and said doctors should ensure that their patients exercise at least thirty minutes a day, five times a week. In the days of the Bible there were no cars, no fast-food outlets, no supermarkets with pre-packaged food, and people didn't need to be told to exercise. They had to walk everywhere and often catch their own food before they could cook it and eat it.

So it's a matter of exercising physically and spiritually. Ask the Holy Spirit to search us and show us (Psalm 139): letting go of negative thinking (being argumentative, always having to be right, being judgmental and critical, being ambitious, not putting others first, not forgiving, and more), and building sound spiritual schemas is not beyond our reach. The Bible has given us all we need – it is our manual, our handbook for life, and God Himself enables us to do it. "God's power has given us everything we need for life and godliness, through our knowing the One who called us to his own glory and goodness" (2 Peter 1:3, CJB). We don't have to wait for a massive haemorrhage to discover these truths because we know them, and we can make sure we are applying them *now*. Jill, a brilliant secular brain scientist, says that through understanding how the two hemispheres of the brain work, she is able to find joy and gratitude at being alive. So how much more should we, who dwell in the Presence of the One who created everything, including every brain in the universe, be able to find those things?

Notes

1. Steven Zarit, "Diagnosis and management of caregiver burden in dementia", *Handbook of Clinical Neurology*, 89 (2008), pp. 101–106.
2. Jill Bolte Taylor, *My Stroke of Insight*, London: Hodder & Stoughton, 2009.
3. Caroline Leaf, *Who Switched Off My Brain?*, Southlake, TX: Thomas Nelson, 2009.
4. Aaron Antonovsky, *Unravelling the Mystery of Health: How People Manage Stress and Stay Well*, 1st edn, San Francisco: Jossey-Bass, 1987.
5. Max Pemberton, *Stop Smoking with CBT*, London: Vermilion, 2014.
6. Jill Bolte Taylor *My Stroke of Insight*, p. 143.
7. Ibid., page 147.
8. Malcolm Gladwell, *The Outliers, The Story of Success*, London: Penguin Books, November 2008.

Chapter 6

A Way to Conquer the Dementia Plague

Science searches for the answer but could it be simply living the way God intended?

> *God's power has given us everything we need for life*
> *and godliness, through our knowing the One who called*
> *us to His own glory and goodness. (2 Peter 1:3, CJB)*

We can charge, and even change, the meaning of things by talking about them differently. Prime Minister David Cameron says that dementia is "the greatest threat to humanity". Sir Terry Pratchett called it "tragedies behind closed doors". Others have said it's "today's most dreaded disease", and one of our residents in the early stages called it her "forgettery". Now two leading academics have likened it to a plague. They say that all the plagues in history were caused by rapid changes in human behaviour and predict that, as with the historical plagues, dementia will be defeated by human ingenuity.

Professor Christopher Dobson is Professor of Chemical and Structural Biology at Cambridge University and Dr Mary Dobson is a historian of medicine specializing in the history of plagues. In a lecture in the Darwin College series on "Plagues and History", they illustrated how the deadly plagues in history were caused as much by rapid changes in human behaviour as by pathogens.[1]

The biggest difference between the plagues of history and the "dementia plague" is that, although it affects large numbers of people, it is not caused by a bacterium or a virus. But it does raise the question of how much it has been caused by changes in human behaviour. And how did Alzheimer's disease, which was only recognized just over 100 years ago, become a modern "plague"? The Cambridge scientists attribute it almost entirely to the fact that we are living longer, thanks to advances in medical science and improvements in public health and standards of living. But in place of diseases that led to early death, the traditional plagues, have come modern, chronic diseases such as cancer and heart disease, though they, too, are gradually being beaten, thanks to major research and better public education. Some of these modern-age diseases are the result of human behaviour, such as alterations in diet and exercising too little. We have eliminated so many common diseases in our lifetimes, but are seeing the emergence of others that are generated by our lifestyles, which are completely different from those of any of our ancestors.

Research into dementia is taking place all over the world. At Cambridge University, scientists are investigating the effects of "misfolding proteins", a phenomenon that happens when protective mechanisms known as "molecular chaperones" fail to prevent it. The chaperones have been knocked out by our living longer and having more than enough food to eat without needing to exercise ourselves to acquire it. In short, changed human behaviour has damaged one of our protective mechanisms. The Cambridge theory is that, as the misfolded proteins lose their normal functions and also clump together, they generate pathogenic agents which progressively damage or destroy the cells in their vicinity. If these damaged cells are in the brain, this phenomenon can give rise to dementia; if they are in our pancreas, to diabetes.

Other studies are looking at different angles. Israeli neuroscientist Professor Illana Gozes and her team are working on drug development to protect neurones, springing from fifteen years of research into a molecular substance, ADNP, which has implications for autism, schizophrenia, and Alzheimer's disease. Also being investigated is the importance of sleep in this high-pressure world. Researchers at the Center for Translational Neuromedicine at the University of Rochester Medical Center in New York have discovered what they call a "microscopic cleansing system" that turns on as soon as we fall asleep and washes the brain clean of cellular waste. The team found that injected amyloid protein disappeared faster from mice brains when the mice were asleep, suggesting that sleep normally clears toxic molecules from the brain. Researchers at Stanford University are looking at another aspect of sleep "healing", involving a single protein called EP2, which stops microglia cells that clear the brain of bacteria, viruses, and dangerous deposits from operating efficiently. Researchers found that blocking EP2 with a drug reversed memory loss and myriad other Alzheimer's-like features in mice. There are dozens of others, too, all looking at solving the problem from different perspectives.

It seems that God is always kind and generous in showing mankind a way out of its self-induced predicaments. Perhaps if the dietary and hygiene laws He gave (Leviticus chapter 11 and Deuteronomy chapter 14) had been followed, most of the plagues in history might have been avoided. I wonder how much difference Mark 12:31 would have made, too.

There's a delightful little account of a time when human behaviour actually helped to stop the spread of a plague, in this case the "Black Death". You may know it already, but I only came across it on the History Learning Site[2] when looking up information about plagues. It isn't about dementia, but it's about the power of human behaviour in changing events, and it's about self-sacrifice. In the sixteenth century the bubonic plague was spreading throughout Britain, working its way outwards from London, the main trading centre. It arrived at the little village of Eyam, in Derbyshire, home to 350 people, in a parcel of material the village tailor received from his supplier in London, which contained fleas. Within a week the tailor was dead, and a few weeks later another twenty-eight had died. The villagers were thinking of escaping to the nearby city of Sheffield, but the church rector, William Mompesson, persuaded them against it, fearing that they might spread the plague to the north of England, which had largely escaped the worst of it. The village decided to cut itself off from the outside world: the people quarantining themselves even though they knew it would mean death for many of them. Food supplies were left by outsiders at the village boundary, and cash in payment was put in a water trough filled with vinegar to sterilize the coins. In this way, Eyam was not left to starve to death, though plague continued to devastate the village. Rector Mompesson buried his own family in the churchyard. By the time the plague ended in November 1666, the little village had lost 260 of its 350 people. Their sacrifice may well have saved many thousands of lives in the north of England. William Mompesson survived, and towards the end of Eyam's ordeal he wrote, "Now, blessed be God, all our fears are over for none have died of the plague since the eleventh of October and the pest-houses have long been empty." We can't imagine the fear and the grief the villagers experienced, and their sacrifice is honoured in an annual memorial service still held every "Plague Sunday".[3]

What complex creatures we human beings are – our behaviour can both bring disaster and help to ward it off. No wonder the Bible tells us to be good to one another, to encourage each other to show love and do good things (Hebrews 10:23–25; Ephesians 4:32).

Globalization – humanity's biggest change

Perhaps the most rapid change in human behaviour, and by far the most significant, is the phenomenon known as globalization. It's been happening gradually for hundreds of years but has been speeded up in the last twenty by the arrival of the internet. Our traditional high streets are disappearing as we purchase more and more online. Local producers have become specialists and global corporations are taking over, and the biggest companies are no longer national firms but multinational corporations with subsidiaries in many countries. The world is now interconnected by trade in a way we could never have imagined even fifty years ago. Some global corporations are more powerful than national governments, with turnovers surpassing countries' gross domestic product (GDP).

Gail Wilson, of the Department of Social Policy, London School of Economics and Political Science, in a paper published in the journal *Ageing and Society*,[4] wrote, "Free trade, economic restructuring, the globalization of finance, and the surge in migration, have in *most parts of the world tended to produce harmful consequences for older people* (my italics). These developments have been overseen, and sometimes dictated by inter-governmental organizations (IGOs) such as the International Monetary Foundation (IMF), the World Bank and the World Trade Organization (WTO), while other IGOs with less power have been limited to anti-ageist exhortation."

But it's about much more than trade and communications. Globalization brings exposure to a common world culture, and we are continually influenced and borne along by the most dominant. It distances customers from suppliers, shifts power bases, and removes accountability. There was a time when we could expect to be answered by a real person when we telephoned a company, but now we're all familiar with the electronic gateway that gives us multiple choices. To bring it to pavement level, a particular gripe of mine is the way my local council insists that households put paper and recyclable items such as yoghurt pots, plastic items, and tin cans into the same black box, so the refuse operative (I can't believe I just wrote that – I mean the dustman!) has to stand alongside the vehicle and sort the recyclable items from the papers at the kerbside. I know this is a trivial, very mundane, complaint, but it could be so easy to rectify. Even so, I asked my council why it has to be done this time-consuming, messy way. The answer was that it's acting on the instructions of the Welsh Assembly Government (WAG).

And to whom does the WAG (this "last bastion of communism in the UK", as one commentator observed) answer in this respect? To the bureaucrats of the European Union, of course, who issued the recycling edicts in the first place. Local political forces are weak when it comes to constraining or controlling globalized forces, be they market-driven or bureaucracy-led. The legislation that led to the redefining of marriage seemed to appear out of nowhere, propelled by an unseen force, but it was a global phenomenon in that it became a major theme in European countries and the USA all at the same time.

Globalization can be a force for good but is often the opposite, eroding local cultures and changing attitudes and behaviour. It has a negative effect especially on older people, particularly in developing countries. Dr Dhrubodhi Mukherjee was a consultant with the World Bank in their Urban Renewal Program in India. He is now Assistant Professor at the School of Social Work at Southern Illinois University. He says that "globalization has contributed to economic wellbeing for many developing nations, but it has reduced 'family' into a *non-viable economic institution for the elderly by promoting urbanized social values of individualism and atomic self-interest*" (my italics).[5]

But, even in developed countries like ours, globalization and changing culture has exacerbated a dislocating effect that is isolating thousands of older people. There has been a decline in the extended family and in local communities, the two theatres in which older people really engage with others, and which keep their minds active. The sense of being valued as part of family culture has also largely gone, bringing insecurity, depression, and isolation. Where people once belonged to a family or known group, say the Llewellyns of Bargoed or the Pevenseys of Cornwall, people are now simply individuals, with no background "halo". And charity Age UK says that nearly 2.5 million people over seventy-five live alone.

Nowhere is this more starkly illustrated than in the Welsh valleys. "Up the valleys" there used to be tight-knit mining communities. People there were never rich but they had a wealth of "belonging". Adults there were aunts and uncles to all the children, and front doors were never locked. One of my pastors remembers growing up in a valley like this. When the steel industry burgeoned in Wales some of the miners left to work in that but many returned to the mine, missing the close companionship. Miners looked out for one another. When the chapels were strong and the singing echoed over the valleys, it must have been like a bit of heaven on earth. Many reasons are given for the closing of the mines (environmental issues were added later), but at the time the main one was that it was cheaper to import coal from overseas. Now the valleys are like ghost lands, with many dispirited, disconnected people, social fragmentation, and high unemployment.

If moods and emotions could be seen from space, there would be vast clouds of them, I reckon, all over the world. In the UK there are around three and a half million people over the age of sixty-five living alone, a figure that includes half of all over-eighty-year-olds. Hit by austerity measures, councils have closed their day centres and curtailed other activities where older people used to meet. Within the first six months of its existence, Silverline, a telephone helpline for the elderly, received over 100,000 calls from older people who had no one else to talk to. Eighty-five-year-old Barbara so longed to hear a human voice that she spent all Christmas Day listening to her answerphone. She began to be lonely after the death of her husband of fifty-six years and losing her only daughter to cancer not long afterwards. "The message kept saying there are no new calls – I kept listening to that – I missed the sound of a human voice," she said.

In some regions in the UK, police are struggling to introduce "No Cold-Calling Zones" because lonely pensioners don't want to put off a sales representative who may be the only person they see for days on end. Every resident on a street needs to agree to the no-go area can before it can be given the go-ahead.[6] But it seems that some pensioners would rather put themselves at risk than be completely isolated. Studies by the major charities for older people consistently report high levels of loneliness and depression.

Kitwood wrote that a poor social environment may actually be damaging to nerve tissue. He wrote that "dementia may be induced, in part, by the stresses of life..."[7] "Thus anyone who envisages the effects of care as being "purely physiological", independent of what is happening in the nervous system, is perpetuating the error of Descartes in trying to separate mind from body. As we have seen, the simple idea that neuropathology causes dementia is unsound. There can be substantial neuropathology with dementia – and there can be dementia without significant neuropathology...

"The standard paradigm takes no account of the way in which brain function is translated into brain structure; it ignores those aspects of nerve architecture that are developmental, and thus closely related to a person's experiences and defences.

"It's absurdly reductionistic to suggest, as some have done, that 'everything in the end comes down to what is going on in individual brain cells'. In very many cases, we find that the process of dementia is also the story of a tragic inadequacy in our culture, our economy, our traditional views about gender, our medical system and our general way of life."

We tend to think of disease as always having a clearly identifiable pathological cause. We like the visible, concrete path from A to B, even if it takes us a while to dig out A. But more and more studies are highlighting the pathways of stress, anxiety, and depression that lead to physical disorders. A ten-year study of the health of 70,000 people, part of the Health Survey of England, found that stress and depression are risk factors for dementia.[8] This is a large and ongoing annual survey. All participants were free of dementia at the start of the study period in 1994, and their average age was fifty-five. Of the 10,000 who died, those with the highest mental distress scores were more likely to have died from dementia than were those who were psychologically healthy. The link between psychological distress and death from dementia was independent of other factors that may raise dementia risk, including smoking, alcohol abuse, or physical ailments such as heart disease or diabetes.[9]

The authors wrote, "Cardiovascular risk factors have been linked with dementia, but the association found in our study remained after controlling for them, thus implicating other explanations for the gradient seen." One possibility, they proposed, is that chronic levels of psychological distress may raise levels of the stress hormone cortisol. Persistently high levels of cortisol, in turn, may have toxic effects on the hippocampus, a part of the brain that is critical for memory. They call for further research to investigate whether appropriate treatment of depression reduces dementia risk. They say that understanding the links between psychological distress and dementia is important, since treatments for depression and anxiety are available and effective. Numerous other studies have joined the dots between negative emotions, raised cortisol levels, inflammatory processes, and physical illness, including dementia.

In a study of 800 women over a thirty-eight-year period, where 104 developed Alzheimer's disease, researchers at the University of Gothenburg, Sweden found that women with high levels of neuroticism (a tendency to more intense emotional reactions) were at greater risk when subjected to high levels of stress – but the risk level was the same as for the others when there was no stress.[10] Researchers at Rush University, Chicago revealed that people with feelings of loneliness are twice as likely to develop Alzheimer's disease.[11] Also, depression causes a reduction in blood flow to the brain.[12] Stress impedes weight loss and can even cause weight gain, according to an American study. In a study by care consortium Kaiser Permanente, 472 overweight adults were put on a diet and an exercise programme designed to help them lose weight. They were first assessed for their level of stress. Researchers found that the most stressed participants lost less weight and – worse – when they became more stressed during the study they actually gained weight.

The effect of negative emotions on dementia sufferers when they have to go into hospital is well known. Their condition deteriorates fast. Anxiety and stress levels rise; they can't make sense of their environment, as it's noisy and confusing with people they don't know, and sometimes they don't understand why they are there. Hospital staff can be kind, but they don't have the time that's needed when dealing with a person with dementia, and they may not have had sufficient training (though that seems to be improving.) More to the point, they don't know the most important thing – *the person inside.* In a community, the person is known. It's so important, because, as mentioned earlier, dementia is a mix of the pathology and *the person.*

Elizabeth was living in her own apartment in our extra-care housing complex, where the domiciliary care team understood her very well. ("Domiciliary" means care provided in an individual's home.) She was a gentle lady, a retired music teacher with a sense of humour that shone even through her dementia – she had expressive, twinkly eyes. She could talk only with difficulty, but managed to say what she wanted if you were patient and relaxed, and, while she didn't dash about at speed, she was fully mobile. Elizabeth's special delight was joining others in the big lounge for meetings and devotions: she loved the talks and the music.

One day the care manager, Georgina, detected a change in her – something she couldn't put her finger on, and which Elizabeth couldn't tell her about. She just wasn't her usual self. Georgina ran tests for urinary tract infection and other possibilities, but found nothing, and Elizabeth ended up going into hospital for investigations. After a few days she had stopped talking, and after a week was not interested in eating. After two weeks she had deteriorated so badly that Georgina consulted with relatives and decided that unless a physical cause was found quickly she would bring Elizabeth back to her own home. The hospital consultant told Georgina that Elizabeth had deteriorated so badly that she was about to be moved to the EMI (elderly mentally infirm) ward, but Georgina stood her ground and said she wanted her back home. The doctor was so surprised that she shook Georgina's hand, and asked if any special equipment would be needed. A full-blooded Scot, Georgina was not one to miss an opportunity, so she thought swiftly and gave a little list, and one of the marvels was an amazing chair – a big padded affair on wheels, which twirled and moved at the touch of a fingertip. So Elizabeth came home, and when I visited a couple of weeks later she was eating and speaking a little (though she never did walk again) and the sparkle had come back to her bright blue eyes. She was clearly very frail, but was quite contented in her own flat with her music and her furniture and pictures in her own sitting room.

Is it possible that, by changing cultures and fragmenting communities, globalization – the most rapid and pervasive change in human behaviour ever observed – has created cultural environments that are causing the psychological symptoms that research shows greatly increase the risk of developing dementia? Is the new global culture that promotes individualism and the "me, me, me" syndrome also producing the malign social pathology that Kitwood described? If that is what is happening then it will affect every one of us. If the bell is tolling for today's older people, then who is going to stop it for us when we reach old age?

Health found in community

People are made for relationship. There's a sense of connectedness among the "people of the book" from the beginning of the Bible to the end. People of the "household of faith" are so interlinked that we're described as being "one body" (Romans 12:5, 6).

The significance for Elizabeth and others in the extra-care housing scheme in Yorkshire is that it is a community. Everyone has their own apartment, and can join in community life as much or as little as they like. The "extra care" comes from a small team of carers who give practical help to people in their own homes there. Perhaps one of the most heart-warming "community" stories I've heard is from a man whose wife had died a few months before we met. He explained that they'd chosen to buy an apartment there because they knew she had a terminal illness that wouldn't need nursing care, but personal (social) care at the end, and they didn't want to be separated by her having to go into a care home. (Social care is the way you'd look after a relative, helping with dressing, washing, cooking, and so on. Nursing care is when there is medical intervention of some kind.) They'd been in their apartment for a couple of years when the illness really took hold. The support was exactly what he'd hoped for, and more. They were able to continue living together, as they'd done all their married life, and because the care team was on site he, too, was supported. He was able to leave his wife on her own in their apartment while he went shopping, for instance, knowing that a carer was only a bell-push away. But the really unexpected blessing was the support and empathy he received from the others after his wife died. It's a Christian community so they shared the same values and beliefs, including what we call "the hope of glory".

When I was growing up in Wales my district had a strong sense of community. Everyone knew each other, to a greater or lesser degree. There were policemen who used to know us, and it was a terrible thing if one saw you doing something wrong and threatened to tell your mother. Welsh "mams" were the power base of communities in those days. Today's mams are all out at work doing their best to earn enough to pay the mortgage, and it seems to be the same all over the world. A survey by Age UK in 2014[13] found that older people felt that they couldn't talk to their neighbours because they were so busy, out at work during the day and then in the evening with housework and so on, and they didn't want to feel that they were a burden. No one knows others in their neighbourhood in the same way, and the spirit of community has largely gone.

Now "community" has come to mean something more ephemeral. Today it could describe the circuit of your life, the place where you work, where you shop, the friends you associate with, your church, and perhaps your social media. It also describes groups of people with common interests, who may live all over the world. Others have defined their communities as "'a group of people that I share values, activities, hopes and dreams with". These are good, but they are elective communities – you choose to join them. But I believe that the communities God designed for human beings were more basic than that. They were places where you lived, with people that you knew. You didn't actually have to like everyone, but communities were places where there were morals, perhaps because behaviour, to a large extent, is moderated by the reactions of people who live alongside each other. Living anonymously next to people you might never know doesn't promote the same kind of moderation. You're more likely to be kept awake by early-morning parties in "anonymous" streets than in a community. This is not to say that communities have disappeared altogether – they still exist in rural and semi-rural areas. And there are still communities where people choose to live with shared commonalities. In Bradford and Leicester, for instance, there are Muslim communities.

A sense of community in American Trader Joe's stores is one of the reasons it's good for your brain, says science writer David DiSalvo.[14] "Of course, it's also down to the employees, who are unabashedly engaged in what they do, including bagging your groceries." In fact, staff do so well that DiSalvo suggests that, instead of sending their staff to business seminars, companies should get them to listen to TJ's employees. But as well as motivated, happy employees, DiSalvo says, "I realize that it sounds quaint to say a store has a communal feel, but walk into a TJ's and the feeling wraps its arms around you. TJ's employees interact like friends working together at jobs they genuinely enjoy."

The headline that caught my eye one morning said that Loma Linda, a place not too far from my family in California, "holds the secret to a long, healthy life". I wondered how that could be, because that part of Southern California has been suffering from a fifteen-year drought and is a hot, dry dustbowl of a place: so dry that people sometimes get nosebleeds, I'm told. But, yes, the article went on to say that Loma Linda "oozes good health".

Approximately 24,000 people live at Loma Linda, and they believe in the importance of a good diet, and good living habits. There was an interview with a 101-year-old lady who goes to the gym and lifts weights, and who credits her long life to a balanced lifestyle, with no drugs, going to bed early, and "praising God for his goodness". "The reason for this extraordinary longevity could be rooted in their faith," wrote the BBC's Peter Bowles. "It is an evangelical Christian community that follows strict guidelines about food, exercise and rest."

People there live up to ten years longer than most Americans, and only develop chronic illness very late in life. "The data is clear, the data has been published, the data has been peer-reviewed," said Dr Wayne Dysinger, chair of the preventative medicine department at Loma Linda University School of Medicine.[15]

Sixty years ago, the data from another community of Italian immigrants in Pennsylvania was so incredible that it was not just peer-reviewed – it was analysed, dissected, disbelieved at first, discussed, and checked exhaustively by teams of experts.[16]

It began in the 1880s, with a trickle of Italian immigrants from a region 100 miles south-west of Rome. By the late 1890s, almost 2,000 had sailed over. They settled on a rocky hillside similar to the landscape they'd left, built houses and a church, and named their town Roseto after the one they'd left behind. They became a close-knit, prosperous community. In the 1950s, a holidaying university lecturer from Oklahoma, Dr Stewart Wolf, was amazed to hear from a local doctor that no one from Roseto under the age of sixty-five had heart disease. At that time heart attacks were the leading cause of death in men in that age group. Wolf enlisted the support of some of his students and colleagues from Oklahoma, and spent the whole of the next summer examining the people of Roseto. They even tracked down relatives of the Rosetans who were living in other parts of the States, but found they did not enjoy the same remarkable health as their relatives in the little Pennsylvania town.

Wolf brought in sociologist John Bruhn to help. They hired medical students and sociology graduate students and researchers and examined not only the community and their genetic inheritance, but the buildings, the soil, the diet, and even the genes of relatives in "their" region of Italy. They examined towns nearby, but none had the same longevity and health in old age as the people of Roseto.

Yet the Rosetans had a diet that would be frowned on today. They ate meat and loved butter and pasta; they cooked with lard, and, in short, ate a lot of fat and carbohydrates. But they had kept the family ties and the close community values they'd brought from the old country. Interviewed by *New York Times* journalist Malcolm Gladwell, John Bruhn remembered, "There was no suicide, no alcoholism, no drug addiction, and very little crime. They didn't have anyone on welfare. Then we looked at peptic ulcers. They didn't have any of those either. These people were dying of old age. That's it."[17]

The researchers concluded that the Roseto community's stable structure, the "emphasis on family cohesion and the supportive nature of the community may have been protective against heart attacks and conducive to longevity". There was much scepticism at first among the wider medical community, but there was no other finding. Conventional wisdom says that our health and longevity depend to a great extent on our genetic inheritance, as well as on our diet and how much exercise we take.

"No one was used to thinking about health *in terms of community*," commented Gladwell. "They had to look *beyond* the individual. They had to understand the culture he or she was a part of, and who their friends and families were ... they had to appreciate the idea that the values of the world we inhabit and the people we surround ourselves with have a profound effect on who we are."

In the 1960s the younger generation of Rosetans grew up and went to college and returned with different values. They abandoned their old community ways for more typically American behaviour – in other words, they adopted the dominant culture of the country. Researchers noted that "the social changes that occurred in Roseto in the 1960s are reflected in sharply increased rates of heart attack among men under the age of 65".

Another remarkable community is Minamisanriku, on the east coast of Japan. It was one of the worst-hit towns in the 2011 tsunami. Homes and livelihoods were completely destroyed. Survivors were housed in evacuation centres or in temporary housing, and everything was done with efficiency and compassion. But there was little incentive to move; to get up and walk. After a while, formerly active people who'd been farmers, fishermen, and businesswomen complained they couldn't walk or get up, and had pain in their backs. They began to say things like, "I used to walk every morning and evening, but I can't do it now"; "My legs are getting weak, so I can't walk or stand up."

Watching his father collecting fresh water one day, a son said, "I always thought he was strong. But when I saw him struggling to carry water like this, I realized he'd aged."

The town's mayor, Jin Sato, called in Dr Yayoi Okawa, an expert in helping to improve life at disaster evacuation sites by focusing on health issues. She identified a deteriorating condition known as "disuse syndrome" and explained, "Every possible function of the body deteriorates in Disuse Syndrome. You have to regard it as something completely different from a normal cold or stomach disorder which you may be familiar with. 'Lifestyle' is the keyword. The treatment method is simple. All that is required is to move your body in your daily life."

But, first, people had to be motivated. Survivors tended to stay inside their temporary housing units. Dr Okawa introduced a community supporter system which involved asking residents to come up with ideas for encouraging them to come out and move their bodies.

The mayor involved not only his staff but the entire community. He said, "Basically, we asked everyone how they could use their particular field of expertise; for example, if you like dancing, you could invite residents out to dance with you, or show them how to dance. Or if you like singing, you could invite residents to join you and enjoy singing together. We worked on ways to bring all those who are suffering from disuse syndrome to come out and do something with other people."

Before the disaster, Chikako Abe used to teach Japanese dance, but stopped after the tsunami washed her house away. When she heard about the community support system she started teaching again. Her oldest student is eighty-one-year-old Sachiko Sugawara. Before the disaster, Sachiko had lived in a two-storey combined house and shop. She had run a bag shop for more than fifty years and had been busy: "Purchasing, meeting wholesalers, receiving goods, displaying them on the shelves… I managed everything by myself," she recalls. The tsunami swept away her business, her lifestyle, and all her relationships. But she began to dance and meet people, and life began to emerge again. Farm fields were provided by Motoko Endo. She said, "Just after the disaster, some elderly people were muttering, 'I should have been washed away'. But now they're gradually recovering their vitality and working earnestly, saying, 'My vegetables grew this big!', and feeling the joy of harvesting they say, 'I can have these for dinner!' They also gradually communicate more with each other, asking, 'When did you add the fertilizer?' or 'When did you sow them?' They're kind of competing with each other in terms of recovering their vigour!"

Fisherman Yoshio Sugawara, who'd never lost his passion for the sea and fishing but thought his working life had been finished after the disaster, began repairing his nets. Six months after getting back into his boat he had fully regained his strength, and now goes out to sea almost every day. The reporter who covered the story, Jason Hancock, said, "Three years and eight months after the disaster, the town's recovery is still ongoing, but many of its residents are managing to restore their health to what it was before the disaster."

Even without natural disasters, inactivity and apathy affect many older people. The Minamisanriku story[18] shows how a caring community can help revive them. The Loma Linda story demonstrates how living in community with shared values leads to a healthier, longer life. The Roseto story is proof that social cohesion protects against heart disease. (Cardiovascular health protects against dementia.) It's also an example of how local values can be overtaken by a wider, dominant culture to the detriment of the community, just as we're seeing with the effects of globalization.

The evidence is that people living in community are healthier psychologically and physically. But globalization has knocked these comfortable Humpty Dumpties off the wall and it seems impossible to put them back together again. We are left with neighbourhoods of disconnected, overburdened families and isolated older folk. There are great swathes of isolated, lonely older people who have fallen below our radar.

Yet it isn't the end of the story. In the next chapter are stories of church workers who are building new networks of support for older people, especially for those with dementia: also a quiet, almost underground work that is restoring community to neighbourhoods, street by street, a new nationwide chaplaincy "seek and find" movement, and ways in which the Government's "dementia-friendly communities" initiative can become deep, lasting reality.

In church this morning we sang how God never gives up, never lets go… The drummer got so carried away with his sticks and cymbals that it looked as if he might propel himself out of his surrounding sound zone. But the fact is that it's true – God never gives up. He changes human behaviour, as Pharaoh found with the Egyptian plagues. Everything good starts with Him, and I believe He will give the wisdom, insight, and understanding that will help prevent dementia. "[For] every good gift and every perfect gift is from above, and comes down from the Father of lights, with whom there is no variation or shadow of turning" (James 1:17, NKJV).

Notes

1. http://www.telegraph.co.uk/culture/hay-festival/10855456/Dont-despair-dementia-will-be-cured.html
2. "Eyam and the Great Plague of 1665", http://www.historylearningsite.co.uk/?s=EYAM.
3. http://www.beautifulbritain.co.uk/htm/outandabout/eyam.htm
4. *Ageing and Society*, 22, pp. 647–663. doi:10.1017/S0144686X02008747
5. *Global Studies Journal*, Volume 1, Issue 3, pp. 21–28. Article: Print (Spiral Bound). Article: Electronic (PDF File; 547.832KB).
6. http://www.telegraph.co.uk/news/uknews/law-and-order/11429360/Lonely-pensioners-dont-want-to-ban-cold-callers.html
7. Tom Kitwood, *Dementia Reconsidered: The Person Comes First*, Buckingham: Open University Press, 2008.
8. Tom C. Russ, Mark Hamer, Emmanuel Stamatakis, et al: "Psychological Distress as a Risk Factor for Dementia Death." *Archives of Internal Medicine*, Vol. 171. No. 20, Nov. 14, 2011.
9. http://www.alzinfo.org/03/articles/diagnosis-and-causes/anxiety-depression-increase-dementia-risk
10. http://www.neurology.org/content/early/2014/10/01/WNL.0000000000000907
11. http://www.rush.edu/health-wellness/discover-health/loneliness-and-alzheimers
12. Kitwood, *Dementia Reconsidered*.
13. http://www.ageuk.org.uk/latest-press/archive/older-people-care-needs-not-getting-help/
14. http://www.forbes.com/sites/daviddisalvo/2015/02/19/what-trader-joes-knows-about-making-your-brain-happy
15. http://www.bbc.co.uk/news/magazine-30351406
16. "The Roseto Effect: A 50-Year Comparison of Mortality Rates", Egolf et al., *American Journal of Public Health*, August 1992, 82(8), pp. 1089–92.
17. Malcolm Gladwell, *Outliers, The Story of Success*, p. 7.
18. http://www.nhk.or.jp/japan311/tmrw3-elder.html

Chapter 7

Communities That Work

Church and other communities helping, with powerful results

For as in one body we have many members, and the
members do not all have the same function, so we,
though many, are one body in Christ, and individually
members one of another. (Romans 12:4–5, ESV)

Every Sunday morning, eighty-seven-year-old Kenneth (name changed) is collected with a few others by minibus from his care home in the Suffolk countryside and taken to church. The minibus collects others from their own homes, too. Care home staff had been a little concerned that Kenneth, who has dementia, might "leg it", as they put it, because suddenly and without warning he would decide to go for a walk, loping at incredible speed across the fields that he knows so well in the Suffolk countryside. No matter how dementia-friendly the church, would he get bored and "do a runner"?

They needn't have worried. At church Kenneth was paired up with a "buddy": someone he knew who would befriend him, sit alongside him, and make sure that he had everything he needed. It turned out that Kenneth is so contented in church that he has never shown the slightest inclination to "leg it", to everyone's relief. He sits throughout the service, joining in when a snatch of a hymn stirs his memory and occasionally falling asleep on his buddy's shoulder during the sermon. If he becomes restless at any point his buddy will take him to the toilet, or offer him a drink from the kitchen, or even walk with him around the church garden before going back inside. But most of the time Kenneth sits, listens, zones in and out, and oozes contentment. He has been a Christian for most of his life and simply being in church, with its rituals, the hymns he's always loved, and its sense of peace, is like being at home. It resonates with the lifelong practices and beliefs at the core of his being: and in that comfortable, long-known environment, the Holy Spirit ministers to his soul. What's true of Kenneth can also be said of the others with dementia in the congregation.

For believers, our church fellowship is our central, core community. It's where we learn, share, make friendships, and find encouragement and support. It's where we worship; where in the truest sense we are known and accepted. But, sadly, most people with dementia stop going to church. They feel uncomfortable, not because their church has changed but because their ability to process information is impaired. They can't quite "compute" what is going on; they forget names and faces and have sudden "blanks", and feel vulnerable outside their own four walls, so they withdraw to the safety of their own home, where they will not be confronted with these alarming "blanks". Kenneth's church didn't want that to happen, and a few years ago began a process that has led to its becoming a truly dementia-friendly church. "Dementia-friendly" is actually rather a weak description – "dementia-embracing" describes it better. Everyone at Kenneth's church has been trained in understanding dementia, including what to expect and how to respond.

It's largely because embedded in the fellowship are a couple with a passion for older people and those with dementia. For several years, Rosie and her husband, David, worked as manager and administrator of the Pilgrim Home in Suffolk. Previously, Rosie had been a district nursing sister in the surrounding towns and villages. Her life changed, she says, when she went on a course on leadership and management in dementia care at the University of Stirling, a world centre for dementia training and research. She stepped down as care home manager to devote more time to her church ministry, and still trains in "Mattering", an approach which raises emotional competence in staff based on the principle that both staff and residents are precious – that they matter. It sounds to me to be the secular equivalent of Ephesians 4:32 (NKJV): "being kind to one another, tenderhearted, forgiving one another…"

Rosie has a mischievous sense of humour. Once she was showing round someone who was considering the home for a family member, and, knowing that a good number of the residents had dementia, the person leaned forward and said sotto voce to Rosie, "Where are they?" With a straight face Rosie answered in the same, conspiratorial manner, "They're all around us!" It was perfectly true. They were all quietly occupied in one way or another. Some liked to rummage in the big bags of coloured material dotted around on coffee tables, some liked to paint or sketch, and some were occupied in other ways. A few years ago I met eighty-two-year-old Lydia, living in an apartment in the sheltered housing wing. She said she loved the view of the beautiful countryside from her window; she thought the home was very well run and comfortable, but complained that there were too many activities every day. "There's something going on all the time!" she protested. "Old people should be allowed to just sit around and do nothing." Older people can have physical frailty and reduced energy levels, but most still like to be occupied, even if it's just chatting with one another, and generally they enjoy activities. Those with dementia need to be drawn out and encouraged to stay engaged with life – especially the Christian life that is so important for their well-being.

Knowing Rosie's passion for dementia sufferers, it would have been odd if their church had not become one hundred per cent dementia-friendly. Even so, nothing is possible unless the leadership is thoroughly behind it. Some may not relish the distraction of people getting up and wandering around, or shouting inappropriately. All our homes are blessed by having preachers from local churches, and I remember hearing about an instance when one of them encountered behaviour he wasn't used to that put him right off his stride. He was in the middle of his talk when Patricia (name changed), a very "proper" little lady who'd clearly been brought up with impeccable manners but now had dementia, got up out of her seat and walked up to where he was standing and positioned herself directly in front of him. She proceeded to scrutinize him intensely from top to toe as though he were an unusual mannequin in a shop window. Her friend went up and, linking her elbow through Patricia's in the friendliest way, led her back to her seat. The poor speaker had not had this happen before, and was not best pleased. It's a good idea to mention to visiting preachers that the church embraces people with dementia.

I mentioned in another book the daughter and father in the States who were looking for an accepting church for him. They tried a few and eventually found one that seemed suitably "laid-back." All was well until, at a point in his sermon, the pastor proclaimed that we were all on a journey, all going home, and her father, catching the pastor's enthusiasm, shouted out, "Home, home on the range!" Without missing a beat the pastor asked the music group if they could play that song. They did, and the whole church joined in. Her father was blessed and affirmed, there was no embarrassment, and everyone was happy. She knew they'd found a church that would be comfortable with him, and him with them. It's an example, too, of how everything cascades from the leadership.

Knowing how many congregations are irritated even by children's noises, I asked Rosie how her church leadership felt about noisy and perhaps shouted-out distractions. She said that the pastor and his wife had six ebullient children and the church was well used to it. But that is only half the answer: once in church and settled into the service, most dementia sufferers tend not to create disturbances. It's not just the peaceful atmosphere, or even the resonance with deep memories and beliefs, but the "holding" presence of God Himself. In his book *The Man Who Mistook His Wife for a Hat*, neurologist Oliver Sacks tells of Jimmie, a man who had dense amnesia and could not remember isolated items for more than a few seconds. Everyone concerned with his care had an overwhelming sense of something missing, and Dr Sacks wondered if he had lost the essence of himself, if he was a spiritual casualty, a "lost soul". He put this to one of the Sisters, who suggested he observe Jimmie during a service in the hospital chapel. There he saw him worshipping, "no longer at the mercy of a faulty and fallible mechanism – that of meaningless sequences and memory traces – absorbed in an act of his whole being, which carried feeling and meaning in an organic continuity and unity, a continuity and unity so seamless it could not permit any break".[1] Welsh pastor Selwyn Hughes, founder of Crusade for World Revival (CWR), believed that in worship we enter into the presence of the Lord and in His unity find our unity. He puts our fragmented, world-weary selves back together.

And, of course, there are the hymns and the music. Much has been written about the effect of music on the brain, especially where there's dementia. Listening to old, well-loved hymns can have a powerful effect on older Christians. Christine, the daughter-in-law of a former pastor now suffering with dementia, is one of many who have told us about how they've seen worship music cut through the fog and touch the soul. The old pastor's dementia was quite advanced and he had lost the ability to speak, so sitting alongside him Christine read some scripture verses and then sang quietly, "Jesus loves me, this I know". She heard him say, "Again", so, surprised, she sang it again, and once more he said, "Again." Then he began to sing it with her, hesitantly at first, and then more confidently. It was not a mindless repetition but an act of worship. His regular carer came into the room and stood still, eyes wide in astonishment.

How they made a dementia-welcoming church

Creating a truly dementia-friendly, or rather "dementia-embracing", church is about much more than adjusting the building – it's about adjusting attitudes and expectations. There are six keys to making a church truly dementia-friendly. The first is that there has to be total commitment on the part of the church leadership and everyone else in the fellowship. If the church leader is half-hearted about it, it won't work. But, happily, we're finding that more and more church leaders want to nurture every one of their flock for as long as possible, and that includes seeing people who've developed dementia still coming to church.

From the first key follows the second, which is simply that the entire fellowship has to be educated about dementia: they have to understand what it is and how it affects sufferers. If there were pockets of dissent dementia sufferers would know it – they would *feel* it. They have heightened emotional awareness. Having said that, most Christians have great compassion for people with dementia and are more confident about being able to help once they have a good understanding of what it is.

Compassion springs from empathy, and this is where the third key turns. It's important to learn from someone who understands how to care for people with dementia, not in an academic way but from experience, someone who can educate and train everyone, from the welcoming hosts on the door to the pastor; including the ladies who make the tea. Rosie says that if the church doesn't have a person with that knowledge then they really do need to find someone who does. Our workshops have helped a number of churches gain this understanding. It helps, too, when churches have nurses in the fellowship. Good nurses are amazing: they're not only carers but managers, in the most natural, almost imperceptible way. And always, where possible, Rosie insists, consult the experts, the people with dementia themselves. Ask them what works for them, and what would help to make life in church easier.

The fourth key is to have a buddy system, where someone who knows the person with dementia will sit next to them and see that their needs are met, whether it's for a glass of water, or to walk around outside for a little while, or for the toilet, or just for reassurance and comfort. Most people with dementia are seated at the back of the hall, so they can go out and come back in without feeling self-conscious or awkward about disturbing the others. As I said, Kenneth feels so comfortable with his buddy that sometimes, during the sermon, he will fall asleep on her shoulder. He looks so peaceful that others in the fellowship have asked the lady if she will be their buddy should they develop dementia. A buddy doesn't have to be the same person every time, but has to be someone the person is comfortable with and who knows them well.

The fifth key is having a "dementia team" with a leader with vision. These will be the ones who will train and support the rest of the church. Team members need to meet to pray, share, and support each other, and to be creative in meeting individual needs. Rosie said, "They will need to reflect on what is working well and what needs to improve. It is very important that those ministering to others with dementia support each other prayerfully and practically, and bring concerns about dementia from the wider church to address and put them before the Lord."

The sixth key is in making adjustments to the building, bearing in mind the changed visual perceptions and difficulty with balance that can occur in Alzheimer's disease. Out go matching carpets and upholstery, and in come contrasting materials. Out go carpets with busy patterns, because someone with Alzheimer's who puts her handbag on the floor won't be able to find it again. There has to be good lighting throughout the building, and clear signage on doors, especially toilet doors. Lavatory walls are best painted in a contrasting colour to the lavatory itself. If steps can't be avoided, put strips of fluorescent tape along the edges, so they can be seen easily. (There's a booklet available from the Alzheimer's Society that gives more detail.)

Rosie believes that dementia sufferers should be included in normal life for as long as possible, which means being in "normal" church services. The church holds special "sunset" meetings in the week but Sunday church services are the same for everybody. She's also noticed that even those with quite severe dementia have lasting memories of their churches, which means that if someone has been to, say, a "predictable" Baptist church, he won't feel at home with the livelier worship of a Pentecostal fellowship. It can work the other way round, of course, as I found from a tiny old lady in a care home in the north.

One of our smaller homes had to close when a raft of new regulations meant investing tens of thousands of pounds in alterations simply to keep it going, when it was already running at a steady loss. Before the home closed, residents were found places in other local Christian homes, and, in an extraordinary coincidence, one in the area happened to have seven vacancies. The manager said they'd never before had so many vacancies all at the same time. It was good that seven old folk who knew each other well were able to move in together. After a while I visited to see how they were getting on. One was the tiny lady in her eighties, who for years had been collected by members of her Pentecostal church near the home that had closed, but now, living on the other side of town, had settled for being taken with others to a nearby Brethren church.

"I do miss the worship," she told me, "but the Holy Spirit never leaves us. They don't worship in the Spirit in this church, but they were singing a hymn the other Sunday and the words suddenly came alive for me and the Holy Spirit fell on me and I dropped back onto my seat. They all thought there was something wrong with me, but I was ever so happy!"

Dementia-friendly communities that go beneath the surface

"Dementia champions" and "dementia-friendly communities" have become buzz terms in the last few years. There has been a run of advertising, newspaper articles, and government announcements. An interesting article in 2013 linked the initiative to a programme that was launched in 2005 in Japan, where one in four of the population is over sixty-five (by 2050, the proportion of elderly people in the Japanese population is likely to be 40 per cent). The aim, in Japan, is the same as that in the UK, to educate the public and to recruit and mobilize volunteer dementia "supporters". The Japanese programme raised four million volunteer supporters within seven years, and they are hoping to have six million by 2017. The British Government's initiative is modelled on the Japanese dementia supporters' scheme, according to Mayumi Hayashi, a Leverhulme early career fellow at King's College London.[2] She wrote, "The search for a cheap means of buttressing dementia care has arguably been the greatest attraction of Cameron's 'befriending' scheme – clearly modelled on the Japanese dementia supporters." The Alzheimer's Society website states, "An economic analysis commissioned... in September 2013 showed that Dementia-Friendly Communities could save £11,000 per person per year by helping people with dementia to remain independent, stay out of care for longer and have a better quality of life."

The British scheme was unveiled in 2013, and aimed originally to recruit a million volunteer "dementia friends" by 2015. That has now been increased by three million. But Ms Hayashi believes that many professionals question how relevant volunteer "friends" are to British needs.

"Many prefer the existing system of Admiral Nurses (similar to Macmillan nurses specializing in cancer care), who give specialist care to dementia sufferers and back-up to their carers. Highly trained, and so relatively expensive, these nurses are employed by the NHS, but their numbers have been affected by public spending cuts."

They may cost money, but, as Rose George (the journalist who was horrified by the poor care her father received) pointed out, when Admiral Nurses are employed they actually cut the overall cost of dementia care. She says that her city, Leeds, has a great dementia-friendly strategy which is trying to improve matters in the teeth of huge financial cuts.

You'll recall that Dr Martin Brunet's plan was for a network of dementia nurses based in GPs' surgeries, serving the community. These too would be more effective than agencies that just refer people on to other services. A worker in a church that wishes it had more money so that it could give more support to families with dementia was dismayed at the £50,000 funding a newly established local agency had received simply to give advice and direction.

With the lack of money for good care and the increasing number of people needing it, the concept of dementia-friendly communities can only be seen as A GOOD THING. If it does nothing else, it will remove the stigma and fear of dementia and replace it with compassion and care. Many Christians have taken it to heart, and some have given up their job to voluntarily champion their local initiative. They've told me about working with local authorities and commercial organizations to provide dementia-friendly lighting, pathways, and signage. They teach others about dementia and how to be kind and supportive to sufferers. Big employers such as Marks & Spencer, Argos, Homebase, and Lloyds Bank have committed more than 120,000 staff to training in supporting customers with dementia, bringing the total number to more than 250,000. That there is such a groundswell of goodwill and kindness, with so many people wanting to help, is like having thousands of little lights shining in the darkness.

Yet all the publicity and all the leaflets and websites ignore something so obvious it's like having the proverbial unwanted elephant in the room. Except that that phrase is normally used when an obstacle is seen but not mentioned. In this case, it seems not to have been seen at all, and I've never found it mentioned: when I brought it up, several dementia champions said they hadn't been told about it. Typical of the narrative they generally receive is the Joseph Rowntree Foundation blog, which says, "Dementia-friendly communities are all about enabling those of us who have dementia to continue as active and confident members of our communities. Faced with a lack of support or understanding, many of us give up the things we love to do out of anxiety, fear or lack of confidence… and we slowly withdraw behind our own four walls."

Could that have been written by a real person with dementia? It is fundamentally wrong on a vital fact: dementia sufferers do not give up things they love because of a lack of support or understanding. If it were only that simple! They give up not because anything outside makes them feel uncomfortable, but because of their own internal conflict. They can't make sense of what is happening around them, and they need the familiar. They can't cope with a lot of noise and they don't like being with a lot of people. There comes a point when most dementia sufferers simply don't want to go outside their own home.

The "withdrawing behind our own four walls" is a recognized symptom that has nothing to do with external circumstances. Psychologist Graham Stokes asks, "Is it surprising that, as memory worsens, a person with dementia wishes to stay at home? For many of us, home is a place of safety and security. With a tendency to get lost or go 'blank' without warning, being out and about is a potential source of fear and dread.

"Such actions not only limit risk, they are also psychologically comfortable, for they reduce the volume of evidence that there is something wrong."[3]

In early-stage dementia, knowledgeable people in friendly communities will make a big difference – and the early stage can last for some years. There will be people like Bill, who came up after a talk and said he had dementia and his local shopkeepers, who knew him well, were marvellous to him.

"I've forgotten how to use money," he said, "so when I go to buy something I just hold out the cash on my hand and they take what they need and I put the rest back." Frank, the husband in Frank and Linda's story, had about six "good" years before he went on to the middle stage.

It could be, too, that if there is a good social environment the disease may be held back. In the "plague" chapter, I mentioned Kitwood's hypothesis that "a poor, social environment may actually be damaging to nerve tissue".[4]

It can also help to avoid the social embarrassment felt by many when they go shopping with their loved one. I heard about a lady at a local fête who went around all the stalls lifting off items and putting them in her bag. Should that happen in a dementia-friendly store, staff would be understanding and sympathetic once they recognized that she had dementia.

But the real need for help – the real *crying* need for help – is when the person has withdrawn and has taken their main caregiver with them. "Role entrapment" is a known factor in dementia caregiver burden. Sufferer and caregiver become isolated and worse – not just out of sight but out of mind, too, and even their church fellowships can forget about them. This is when dementia-friendly champions and communities could make a real difference – all the difference in the world.

If the befrienders and champions have developed good relationships with them before they withdraw, then they will be able to help them in a very real way at the time when it matters most. Even staying with Dad while the daughter goes shopping or has her hair done would be a great help. Or people from church visiting regularly to see what prayer requests can be taken back, or asking what needs to be done, such as cutting the grass or helping with filling in forms.

And there are always forms. They exist, in part, to serve the parallel universes that have become endemic to life in this century. Every enterprise seems to have separate streams of people working in these parallel universes, except perhaps Google, which seems to be a shifting kaleidoscope of several. Nowadays medical professionals work with patients to investigate, to diagnose, and to "deliver" the treatment, and alongside this "real" work is a system consisting of managers, computer and management systems, paper forms with tick boxes, budgets, and forms. As the Mid Staffs hospital tragedy showed, the latter can be showing excellent results even while patients are dying in their hundreds. Commenting on an article in a national newspaper, a hospital consultant wrote that, despite his position in his hospital, he was not able to ensure that his father received good care. "Every box can be ticked, and the hospital will be seen to be reaching its objectives, but patients can still be receiving appalling care," he wrote. In the Mid Staffs hospital, where hundreds of elderly patients died in dreadful circumstances, the parallel universe had dominated the real one, decimating medical and nursing staff to the point where they weren't able to work properly. The pathway to hope here is that staff members who spoke to the media after the debacle had been exposed really do care. One nurse said, "I used to go home crying."

Our housing and care home managers are familiar with the entire dementia journey. As well as older people who come in with dementia, there are those who come in because of physical frailty and may develop it later. Once a year these managers get together for updating and fellowship, and over coffee this year I began to ask what their thoughts were on this topic. I got no further than saying "Dementia-Friendly Communities" when their expressions and shaking heads cut me off.

"They're not going to work," said one (a manager for twelve years).

"I don't think it's been thought through properly," said another (with fifteen years' experience).

Yet it *could* work. I discussed it with Sally, a pastoral worker in a large church in Southbourne. She runs a number of projects for older people, including the dementia-friendly community project. She is energetic and indefatigable. One of the clubs she runs, very successfully, is for the "afters", for those who are trying to pick up their social lives again after years of isolation and caring. They were all going to the cinema one day when I called. If dementia-friendly communities succeed in helping at the point where help is really needed, where it is life-changing, it will because of people like Sally, who will be prepared to go down the rabbit holes after sufferers and caregivers have bolted down them.

There are such communities where Sally lives, and she told me a couple of stories that are so heart-warming they're worth sharing. She takes services in a local care home, and one day a resident said that she'd just been diagnosed with dementia and although she loved to go for a walk she had become too nervous to go because she had begun to get lost and not be able to find her way back. Sally arranged for someone to accompany her, so she is still enjoying her walks. She had also been a French teacher and still enjoyed conversations in French, so one of the befriending team who happens to be a fluent French speaker now visits to have conversations in French.

The other story is about two brothers who travelled from a distance to visit their mother, who had moved into a local care home. One of the things they found she needed was new underwear, so they went into a local shop called, appropriately, Marjorie Daw, which sells clothes from a past era for people who still like old-fashioned garments. The brothers hadn't thought to bring a sample with them and weren't really able to describe what they wanted. They probably thought they'd see what they wanted on display, as you do in Marks & Spencer. The shop owner gave them a handful of different types and sizes to take back to their mother, so they could see what she liked and then return with the rest to the shop and buy a supply of her choice. "Marjorie Daw" didn't ask for their names or even for money. She sympathized with their predicament and knew that they would be back, because she still had a community mindset.

Rebuilding links – a house at a time

"No one cares about us round here. Years ago, everyone knew each other. What we need to bring us together is a coffee morning!" These were the words of an elderly lady in a group of council bungalows reserved for older people, responding to a knock on the door and an introduction by Colin Johnson, a Neighbourhood

Chaplain in Bedfordshire. After meeting this lady he got a few volunteers together and started a coffee morning. The numbers grew month by month until there were over twenty-five coming together in the St John Ambulance Hall.

Colin believes in neighbourhood visiting. He finds two or three people in every street who want to keep in touch and are happy to receive the church's Christian newspaper and other information.

"When I call on a new street, my first comment is, 'I'm from the local church and I'm calling as a good neighbour,'" he says.

Over the years he made so many contacts that it was difficult to keep up with them all, so he began to ask Christians in neighbouring churches to help with befriending and the odd practical task. And from that grew the idea of a network of Neighbourhood Chaplains.

There are three Christian organizations involved in the developing scheme – the Association of Christian Counsellors, Christian Charity Counties, and the London School of Theology. It will be patterned on what has worked so well for Colin. The lead chaplains will make the first neighbourhood contacts, and a befriender team will follow up with those who would like friendship or to have someone from the Helping Hands team to do small jobs, such as cutting the grass.

It is not intended to be a "one-size-fits-all" programme. Colin sees three types of Neighbourhood Chaplain scheme emerging: one for small groups of Christians working with their local church, another that is adopted by the whole church where all the different gifts and skills in the church family are engaged, and yet another that is run by several churches in a local community. There will also be training, especially in setting boundaries and "safeguarding", as teams will find themselves working with vulnerable groups, such as those with disabilities, dementia, and other health problems.

Colin said, "It is inspiring to see how Jesus sought people out, looking for those who were the outcasts as well as those who were part of the in-crowd. Jesus is eager for us to imitate Him and to give our lives gladly to love and serve non-Christians." Neighbourhood Chaplains will first build bridges in the love of the Lord and then naturally take the gospel to those who will hear it. Colin is Neighbourhood Chaplain with Hockliffe Street Baptist Church, Leighton Buzzard, and his email is Johnson@ countiesuk.org.

Restoring community – a street at a time

For some time a quiet revolution has been taking place in our towns and cities, with the concept of community street by street. A couple from Birmingham, Martin and Gina Graham, wanted to restore healthy values to society in the UK, and saw the answer as bringing them back at grass-roots level by drawing together communities. For many years they had run an evangelical organization called "On the Move", which used to operate by bringing churches together to hold free barbecues. There would be music groups in the streets handing out invitations and hundreds would accept and go along. Dozens of churches in an area would come together beforehand and be trained by the On the Move team, and they would organize the barbecues together, too. There would be worship music and testimonies, and then volunteers would move around the tables asking guests what they thought of it, and what they would like prayer for. Thousands not only came to faith but were "churched" almost straight away. The story of On the Move is told in the book *Sizzling Faith*.[5] Before that, Martin was chief executive of the Kent Chamber of Commerce, one of the largest in the country.

In 2010 Martin and Gina set up the Community Interest Company, Uturn UK CIC, and have been running the Street Associations initiative since then. "Wherever you live in the UK, a Street Association offers a simple catalyst to get community spirit back – and a framework to keep it going. And we offer everything you need to introduce it to your street," says Martin. "Many people feel rather shy about taking the initiative in their street. But they also feel that it's such a shame when people live so separately, leaving many isolated, the generations hardly mixing, ethnic groups left out, vulnerable people unsupported – and a huge amount of friendship and fun missed out on, all because somehow we're not supposed to invade people's 'private space' any more!" But, Martin encourages, "The good news is that the idea of a Street Association will receive a huge welcome on your street, from many people who feel as you do. It just needs someone to light the blue touchpaper!"

Lighting the flame couldn't be simpler: Street Associations provides a stock letter which can be personalized and hand-delivered, inviting neighbours to meet; and, a week later you host a meeting and put on the kettle. There's also a step-by-step guide for introducing the concept, a seven-minute video to show at the meeting, which explains everything, window stickers for everyone to put up along the street, and lots of ideas on how to take it forward.

Street Associations work in partnership with Neighbourhood Watch and the Big Lunch, an initiative of the Eden Project. The Big Lunch team are encouraging "Big Lunchers" to set up a Street Association so that a once-a-year event can become an ongoing expression of community building through the year. They're also working closely with a number of local authorities, who would like to see Street Associations in their area, usually with an element of financial support.

Amanda is a part-time social worker, with three boys aged between two and nine. She has been part of the core group since its inception two years ago. She writes, "Being part of the Street Association has given me more of a sense of where I am. It's given me the confidence to say hello to people I meet on the street. We all lack the confidence to go up to someone and suggest meeting for tea, but I've been so warmly received by so many nice people that I can actually do it now. You also feel you can ask a neighbour if you run out of something." She adds that knowing who lives on the street gives her the confidence to let her nine-year-old son go to the park on his own. Amanda's last comment says so much in just a few words: "I know it's not about doing things to feel good, but it was such a good thing to give a lift to and from the Street Association Christmas party to an elderly man and his wife, who suffers from dementia. They had a great time and it turned out to be the first time they'd been able to go out as a couple for years."

Dyllis, eighty-seven, lives alone and is partially sighted. She moved into the street in 1980, but says that the year following the launch of the Street Association was special.

"People now speak to me. The other day, Kumar said to me:

'Before the first Street Association meeting, we'd have walked past you; now we stop for a chat!'

"I've got to know ten or twelve people well. The street feels different now. There's no feeling of isolation. If in need, I could knock on a door for help. There was a power cut, which was scary, but a neighbour who I got to know through the Street Association came immediately with a torch and candles – my knight in shining armour!"

Street Associations are good for everyone, but they're especially great for older people. Martin tells of a couple posting leaflets through doors and meeting an elderly gentleman who hadn't left his home for over a year, because he was his wife's sole caregiver. You can see a video of a typical street, with people describing their own experiences, at: https://www.bvt.org.uk/our-communities/street-associations. There's also a contact box, if you are interested in having one on your street.

Living in community influences the way people think about each other. There are around 10,500 parishes in England and Wales, many of which are fairly small neighbourhoods. Traditionally found in every parish was the church (or two), the pub, the village green at the centre, and, usually somewhere in the middle, the solid red British telephone box. Practically indestructible and with a distinctive design, they were as much a part of British life as Cadbury's chocolate, London buses, and fish and chips. With the advent of mobile phones they became redundant and were decommissioned. The phones were removed, but many of the boxes remained. But they didn't just stand and moulder: more than 1,500 have been bought by local parishes, repainted and shelved, and turned into miniature voluntary libraries. They made the news when an inspector from the notorious health and safety regulator declared that the books were a hazard. One of them might fall and hurt someone. (We'd better close all our libraries, then, wrote one commentator.)

In its editorial column, *The Daily Telegraph* said that the interesting thing about this tale wasn't the preposterous health and safety nonsense. "We are used to that." No, it was the inspiring aspect that all over the country parish councils have taken over the "attractive little structures" and turned them into voluntary libraries. "What spring sunshine is to dark matter, these phone boxes are to vandalism. It is very cheering." Yes it is, because the phone boxes are evidence of how people in community want to "do good" to one another.

Notes

1. Taken from *The Man Who Mistook His Wife for a Hat* by Oliver Sacks, London: Picador, 2009.
2. http://www.theguardian.com/society/2013/jun/11/dementia-lessons-from-japan-hunt
3. Stokes, G. *Challenging Behaviour in Dementia: A Person-Centred Approach*, 2014.
4. Kitwood *Dementia Reconsidered*.
5. Martin Graham, *Sizzling Faith*, Eastbourne: Kingsway, 2006.

Chapter 8

Connecting at the Eternal Level

The Holy Spirit connects us even when other communications fail

Deep calls to deep in the roar of your waterfalls...
(Psalm 42:7, NIV)

One of my iconic pictures is of a church visitor talking to a resident with dementia. The visitor was touching her hand, and looking directly into her eyes. The resident's face was aglow and radiating so much joy that I stopped to see what the visitor was saying. She was quietly reciting Proverbs 3:5, and, whether or not the resident could understand the words, she was clearly understanding the message. Taking out my camera, I introduced myself and asked if I could take a photograph. The visitor said yes and the resident responded with a sentence of soft gibberish, but it was clear that she was saying yes. She had turned her face towards me and her body was relaxed – communication signals that we interpret intuitively hundreds of times each day.

Communicating involves so much more than words. It happens in dozens of other ways – with gestures, facial and body expression and kinesics, even the personal space we put between ourselves. Some facial expressions, such as smiling and frowning, seem to be universal and innate. There are photographs on the internet at the moment showing a baby in the womb grimacing as its mother smokes a cigarette. Gestures and body language can vary between cultures: when we lived in the Middle East, the habit among some nationalities of nodding their heads up and down to indicate "no" and from side to side to say "yes" was confusing till I got used to it. There's also a kind of mini-head roll that says "maybe". Combined with big, expressive eyes, their meanings were always clear. In America, an arm over your shoulder can mean a kind of bonding: "You're one of us," or "You're safe with me," or even approval, but in the UK it's more often to comfort and reassure. This might explain why, during an official visit, the Duchess of Cambridge almost froze in place when a famous American sportsman put his arm around her shoulders.

Something that we take for granted, but which is very important, is the language of touch. "The lack of platonic touch in men's lives is a killer," according to writer Mark Greene ("The Good Men Project"),[1] leaving them "physically and emotionally isolated. Cut off from the human physical contact that is proven to reduce stress, increase self-esteem, and create community". In his book *Touching: The Human Significance of the Skin*,[2] anthropologist Ashley Montagu writes, "The communications we transmit through touch constitute the most powerful means of establishing human relationships, the foundation of experience…" Nursing and care journals carry articles on the importance of touch, especially for older people and those with dementia. My colleague Janet says that it's impossible to be with people with dementia without feeling their touch.

"You'll be standing, talking to someone, when you feel your arm being stroked, she said. "It will be someone wanting to make contact with you and they want you to know they're there. And it can be their way of saying they appreciate you."

Perhaps the most important means of communicating is just being with others, just going alongside them and "being there" for them. Job's friends were wonderful comforters until they began to speak, when they said the wrong things. A long time ago I read a small book on grief in which the writer told how, some weeks after his wife had died, one of his friends had travelled across the country to be with him, simply turning up on the doorstep because he'd known that if he'd suggested it the writer would have told him not to bother to come all that way. One sentence said so much: "We didn't speak much; just walked and smoked our pipes, and although we didn't talk of Christ He was as much in the air around us as if He'd been visible."

It's sad when people stop visiting dementia sufferers. It sometimes splits families when relatives stay away. It can be very hurtful for the main caregiver. Janet is a pastoral worker who cared for her mother until she reached the stage when she need to go into a care home (for the concentrated care that only teams of trained carers can give). She wrote:

> I think my overwhelming experience of dementia
> is summed up in one word: loneliness. I watched as
> friends gave up on her, some people even to the extent
> of no longer trying to have a conversation; it was
> as if she wasn't in the room. One person said, "It's a
> shame she's lost her personality," because she was no
> longer able to reminisce over shared memories. Even

> *healthcare professionals at medical appointments*
> *didn't seem to know how to cope. At times I felt it was*
> *me and her against a world that didn't understand or*
> *seem to want to.*

Yet believers are bearers of the most powerful means of communication imaginable, because we carry within us the Holy Spirit – we are temples of the Holy Spirit, the Bible tells us (1 Corinthians 6:19). Jesus was very clear about this, telling His disciples that when He left them, after the cross, He would ask the Father to send them the Holy Spirit, who would guide and help them, and remind them of all Jesus had told them (John 14:26).

The Holy Spirit is the ultimate communicator. He tells us things about God, ourselves, and one another – an example being the resident with dementia who wouldn't settle and her friend's astonishment when she prayed for a matter that the friend had kept to herself and which no one knew about. Another example is the story of Mary visiting her cousin Elizabeth, in Luke's Gospel (Luke 1:41). When Elizabeth heard Mary's greeting, it says that Elizabeth's baby "leaped in her womb, and Elizabeth was filled with the Holy Spirit" (Luke 1:41).

Deep calls to deep, the Scripture says (Psalm 42:7). "Only a call from the depths can provoke a response from the depths," Watchman Nee wrote; "nothing shallow can ever touch the depths, nor can anything superficial touch the inward parts. Only the deep will respond to the deep. Anything that does not issue from the depths cannot touch the depths."[3] In *The Problem of Pain*, C. S. Lewis writes, "You may have noticed that the books you really love are bound together by a secret thread. You know very well what is the common quality that makes you love them, though you cannot put it into words..."[4] Although Lewis is describing books here, he could just as well be talking about Christians. Wherever we go, whatever country we live in, whatever denomination we subscribe to, we are bound together by a secret thread: something that is deep within us.

The Holy Spirit is the most powerful communicator in the universe. A couple of years before the dictator Ceauşescu was deposed, two friends and I took Bibles to Romania for a Christian family there to distribute to others. It was a time when Bibles were strictly banned and foreign visitors were suspected and followed by the secret police, although one who followed us one day was so obvious that, had we not been so nervous, we would have laughed. (In those days the fear in the air was almost palpable.) But, in Hungary, driving to the Romanian border along a narrow country road without a building in sight, our car blew a gasket and suddenly there was engine oil all over the windscreen. We lifted the bonnet and the engine was blanketed in it too, and even the ground beneath. We were stunned. We knew we hadn't passed a garage for hours and we had no choice but to go on, so we waited for the engine to cool down and set off again, very gingerly, listening for ominous sounds from under the bonnet. Thank God, about a mile or so up the road there was a workshop and garage. The owner's eyes sparkled at the sight of our European car. We knew he was a true mechanic when he took out our tools (which were metric while his were still imperial) and handled them reverently. The challenge was that he spoke only Hungarian, and between us we could muster only French, German, and Arabic, so we conversed in mime. He indicated it would take an hour to repair, so we went for a walk, found a wall, and sat on it and prayed. When we went back we found the car repaired, the engine and the windscreen clean, and a smiling mechanic who showed us how he had cannibalized a gasket from his stock to fit our engine. I don't know who was the most pleased, him or us! So I took out my wallet and gestured "How much?" but he wouldn't accept any payment at all. A miracle, you might think. But no, he said, he had two sons, one twelve and one fourteen years old, and asked if, when we got back to England, we would send them some milk chocolate. It seemed that milk chocolate wasn't easy to obtain then in Hungary. (He wrote down his address and, when I got back to Cambridge, I sent a box full of the best chocolate I could find.) We were about half an hour up the road from the garage when it struck us that I'd been speaking in English and he'd been speaking in Hungarian and yet we had all understood every word. It was astounding, but it seemed so ordinary at the time. Before writing this I checked with one of the friends who'd been on the trip, a no-nonsense A level RE teacher called Fran. She remembered the incident well, exactly as I've told it. (Hats off to Fran: she's a superb navigator, and had it not been for her exceptional skill we'd still be driving around Romania.) I'm not saying that the role of the Holy Spirit is as foreign-language interpreter, though one of the gifts of the Spirit *is* interpretation (1 Corinthians 12:10), but that He communicates in ways beyond our understanding.

Christians are bearers of the most powerful means of communication imaginable. So when we visit people with dementia who have lost the ability to communicate, who have withdrawn into their own inner world, we have the power of "simply being" alongside them, knowing that we are carrying the Holy Spirit within us. When we do this we are connecting at an eternal level. Christine Bryden, the author I mentioned earlier who suffers with dementia, gave a talk at an international conference in New Zealand some years ago. Part of it was a powerful plea not to give up on people with dementia, but to keep them company – to stay alongside them. With permission, I extracted this part and "set" it as a poem for publication. Christine said:

> *As I lose an identity in the world around me,*
> *which is so anxious to define me by what I do and say,*
> *rather than who I am,*
> *I can seek an identity by simply being me, a person*
> *created in the image of God.*
> *My spiritual self is reflected in the divine and given*
> *meaning as a transcendent being…*
> *As I travel towards the dissolution of myself, my*
> *personality, my very "essence",*
> *my relationship with God needs increasing support*
> *from you,*
> *my other in the body of Christ.*
> *Don't abandon me at any stage, for the Holy Spirit*
> *connects us…*
> *I need you to minister to me, to sing with me,*
> *pray with me, to be my memory for me…*
> *You play a vital role in relating to the soul within me,*
> *connecting at this eternal level.*

Sing alongside me, touch me, pray with me, and
reassure me of your presence,
and through you, of Christ's presence.
I need you to be the Christ-light for me,
to affirm my identity and walk alongside me.

In another context she added:

I may not be able to affirm you, to remember who
you are or whether you visited me. But you have
brought Christ to me. If I enjoy your visit, why must
I remember it? Why must I remember who you are?
Is this just to satisfy your own need for identity? So
please allow Christ to work through you. Let me live in
the present. If I forget a pleasant memory, it does not
mean that it was not important for me.

Visiting people with dementia

One of the most poignant phone calls I've received was from a
retired vicar in his early eighties, who asked if he could make
eight photocopies of *Worshipping with Dementia*. He was one
of a group of retired people in his district who were visiting
people with dementia in care homes, and they'd found the
book, with its short themes and prayers and old hymns, very
helpful. He'd begun when his wife had to go into the care home
with dementia. He explained that they'd looked up the cost of
the book and found that they couldn't really afford to buy eight
copies, but we sent them to him anyway. We were delighted to
be able to bless this faithful pastor's heart. Others have told us
how helpful they find the book, but this was the only time we've
ever been asked about photocopying it.

Genuine love and concern is what counts when visiting people with dementia, whether in care homes or in their own home. Emotions are heightened as cognitive function fails, as I've already mentioned, and it's love that makes its way through and to which hearts will respond. Your good "vibes" will be picked up and dementia sufferers will feel much better as a result of your visit. Your peace will be there also, even though you may not be aware of it. Jesus said, "Peace I leave with you; my peace I give you" (John 14:27). And that peace can be passed on to another person (as Jesus taught in Luke 10:5–6).

There seem to be three main challenges when it comes to visiting people with dementia, even for close relatives. The first is when the person doesn't recognize who you are. It's not uncommon to hear someone say, "What's the point? He doesn't know who I am any more." But, as Christine said, the visit isn't about *you*, it's about the dementia sufferer. And, despite the Government's slogan "Living well with dementia," the fact is that it is a disease and people do suffer with it, and becoming apathetic and withdrawn is one of the ways. But remember, *the person remains,* and it's good if he or she can be drawn out, persuaded even, into interacting.

The second challenge is learning to converse: we're so used to the question-and-answer format that we find it difficult to hold a conversation in any other way. "How are you?" is automatic with us. Avoid asking questions, and especially the irritating rising inflection at the end of a sentence that implies an interrogation when there isn't one. Being asked a question prompts an instinctive response, and for people with dementia this can be challenging and unsettling. It goes without saying that you should speak clearly and evenly, and without raising your voice – unless the person is deaf and doesn't have their hearing aid. Also, keep it simple – keep to one topic at a time.

Thirdly, when the person does converse, they may say things that are puzzling, because sometimes they can use only the words that are available to them. But don't contradict! Listen intently to what they are trying to say and, if appropriate, repeat what they have said back to them but substituting what you believe are the right words. If at times they are struggling to find a word then you could wait a moment and then suggest one, being careful not to interrupt or appear to be impatient.

There may be questions that visitors won't know how to answer at all, such as a ninety-year-old asking when her mother will be coming to collect her. It does her no good at all to hear that her mother died years ago: the best way to respond is by deflecting and diverting. Janet said to a resident, "Our mothers are so important to us, aren't they? Let me tell you about my mother…" Or, knowing that the mother was a believer, she would feel confident in saying, "I'm so looking forward to meeting your mother. Tell me about her!" With practice, you can develop dozens of ways of empathic deflecting. Heaven is a good topic to talk about! It is the "joy set before us" (Hebrews 12: 1, 2).

Before your visit, find out as much personal information as you can about people that you'll be meeting, perhaps enough to cover one side of a letter-size sheet of paper. What were their interests in life? Did they like gardening, or cooking, or photography, for instance? Finding out as much as you can about their interests and their past helps you bring things into the conversation that can bring back memories and feelings. It can also inspire a sense of renewed identity: things that they can hook into and which will make them come alive again. You could take in photographs of the era they grew up in, or fabrics, or cakes you've baked, or sea shells. Knowing a little about their childhood, their wartime experiences, their work, and their achievements and talking about these things can help restore a sense of worth, and reawaken zest. And, for the listener, this can actually be quite fascinating. Sometimes schoolchildren visit residents in our homes to interview them about their past lives, and they find it quite captivating. It is usually memory of more recent events that is lost, so focus on their earlier life, of which the memory can be surprisingly good. Don't forget to find out, too, whether they need reading glasses or hearing aids, and when you visit make sure that they are wearing them.

Always approach a person with dementia from the front, so they can see you coming, and be sure to sit facing them, making good eye contact if possible. Dr Jennifer Bute (the GP we mentioned earlier, who retired early because of dementia), talks about friends and visitors providing the "rungs on the ladder of her memory", allowing her to continue with conversations. It's the same in ordinary circumstances – how many times have you met someone whose face you remember but not the context in which you know them? So remind the person how you know them and of any connections, such as being in the same church or being a neighbour. And remember the power of the Scriptures. Why stress the Scriptures? Because they are "active and living" and have a lasting, beneficial effect (Hebrews 4:12).

Gently chat and throw out conversational hooks that will help stimulate interest and response. If the person is able to converse, allow plenty of time for a response. Other ways to trigger deeper memories are reminders of familiar things such as a favourite song, a hymn, a scripture, or a picture of something from the past that will be recognized. Of course, again, you need to know what these triggers are – but you will be rewarded many times over for your effort if you can awaken old feelings through these much-loved memories. You will feel you are getting through! And, if you bring a scripture verse, bring it in the version that they will have been brought up with (probably the King James Version). Just being there may be enough, and reading Scripture will bring peace, hope, and encouragement – as Christine said, you are bringing a connection with eternity. If you are visiting from the same church, bring news of people and the things that are happening.

Words may not be the most important thing. Some people with dementia are content just to "be", in your presence, without needing to feel they have to come up with words that may be difficult for them to find! Holding hands can be welcomed by many (ask the caregiver about this in advance) and let your warmth be expressed in your body language and your genuine concern. This will minister, even if you think it isn't doing anything.

Don't forget the caregiver

Sometimes, the person with the greatest need in the house you are visiting is the main caregiver. They can be very cut off as a result of the responsibility they are carrying, and they might miss people they can have a normal conversation with. Do give them the attention and respect they deserve, rather than expecting them to be a "fly on the wall" who happens to be present during your visit. Many caregivers are deeply upset by the lack of attention paid to them by relatives and doctors, when they are, in fact, playing the key role in the person's care and well-being. Several caregivers have told us that they actually expected to be ignored, because they weren't the "patient". Also, be sensitive to their mood. Sometimes, trying to jolly someone along can ignore the need of the moment: we are told to "rejoice with those who rejoice; mourn with those who mourn" (Romans 12:15).

But, for a believer, even in the deepest grief there is hope. Marianne committed her life to Jesus at the age of twenty-five and had grown into a mature faith when her husband died of cancer when they were both sixty-seven. She was standing in the church hallway talking to the vicar just before they were to enter the main auditorium for the funeral service when she was suddenly struck by a bolt of doubt so profound it felt like a physical blow to her back.

"What if we've all made a mistake?" she asked the vicar. "What if we're all wrong?" There was no time for a learned exegesis. The Holy Spirit gave him exactly the right answer.

He said firmly, "Marianne – they never found His body. They never did find it."

The vision of eternity is part of the hope that carries us. It still carries Bill Wilson in New York, the pastor at Victory Church, Cwmbran, the former homeless alcoholics and drug addicts, and the millions of other believers who live their lives with a divine perspective. It takes people through the most harrowing circumstances and griefs. Jean is a doctor married to a chemical engineer, both quietly spoken academic types. Their first child, a son, was born with a mysterious syndrome which meant that he didn't develop properly. He was a handsome little boy with a thatch of strawberry-blond hair, but he never walked, or talked, or did any of the things little boys do. His face would light up when his mother dropped little kisses on his forehead, or his father read stories to him. His mother was determined that somehow, at some point, there would be a breakthrough, and they tried everything in their power, including physical therapy and stimulation, different foods, a TV screen over his bed, pushing him in a purpose-made exercise bike that supported him and moved his legs, and they even fixed a special swing on the branch of a big old tree in the garden. They read stories of similar children and their development and constantly urged friends, church, and family to pray and to keep on praying.

When William died at the age of eight everyone worried about how his parents would cope, especially his deeply sensitive mother. But she sent her mother-in-law an email that read, "Actually, I am shocked at how normal I feel. Every time I am tempted to worry that I feel too good, I thank God for His grace. About once every day or two something will make me mist up, but it passes in a moment. Last night I found an entry on a calendar about William smiling in his swing while the golden oak leaves showered down around us. I remember that day. He had only just begun to smile. I thought I would need a full six weeks to stop crying continuously and even then be seriously crumbly around the edges and barely able to work. I am back at work and laughing as usual. God is Good! I hate to admit it, since I did not feel 'burdened' by William when he was alive, but I feel as if a heavy weight has been lifted from me. I think it is because I lived in fear of his death and my inability to cope with it, as I had never lost anybody close to me before. His grace is sufficient for me. I will run the race set before me and be nothing but joyous at the finish line."

Experiences like Jean's remind us that what carries us is not a wishy-washy kind of hope, but something that has *substance*. It carries us because it's not just us reaching for something *out there*, but a projection of something that's *in here, in each* believer. It's Christ in us, the hope of glory (Colossians 1:27). That's why connecting at the eternal level is so important for believers with dementia.

Notes

1. http://goodmenproject.com/featured-content/megasahd-the-lack-of-gentle-platonic-touch-in-mens-lives-is-a-killer/
2. Ashley Montagu, *Touching: The Human Significance of the Skin*, New York: Harper & Row, 1986.
3. http://www.thelastdays.net/deep0.htm
4. C. S. Lewis, *The Problem of Pain*, London: William Collins, 2012.

Chapter 9

The Highway Through the Heart

Caregivers caring for themselves

Blessed are those whose strength is in you,
in whose heart are the highways to Zion.
(Psalm 84:5, ESV)

"We wouldn't have started from here," begins the blog of a caregiver. It puts me in mind of the tourist in Ireland asking a local man if he could tell him how to get to his next destination. The Irishman said he could tell him alright, "but you can't get there from here". The starting point was a few miles distant, and once the tourist got to that point the journey was straightforward. (It was an Irishman who told me this story!) Dementia catches you right where you are, and the road we are on as believers is the "road of blessing" mentioned earlier, the one that runs through the heart. Although it's invisible, it's the most important highway in the world. It's well lit, too: "Your Word is a lamp for my foot and a light to my path," says Psalm 119:105. And among the blessings when you belong to a church fellowship are others who've navigated the tricky bits and can help you with them.

At a workshop, caregivers were asked what advice they would give to others about to start the journey. They were silent, looking thoughtful, and after a minute or two an elderly man spoke up.

"I would say to them that they need patience," he said. "I cared for my wife until she went into a home. I never used to have patience, but I do now." He paused, and then added, tremulously, "I feel I'm a better person for it." I learned afterwards that he had been known for his rather combative contributions among others, including his house group, but that he was now, indeed, a changed man. It's the principle that Pastor Joel Osteen observed with David when he said in Psalm 4:1, "God enlarged me in my time of distress." He didn't get enlarged in the good times, said the pastor; he was increased in the tough times.

This awareness of personal growth usually comes when the caregiving role has finished, after bereavement. While they were still caring, many family members felt frustrated, grieved, stressed, all those emotions mentioned previously – but mainly inadequate. How could they not? It's like trying to keep a melting snowman smartly dressed – no matter how much you adjust the hat or the scarf or the coat, it keeps melting and losing its shape. You may think it's fixed for a while then, suddenly, another bit goes. A wife said, "I went to our doctor and asked him, 'What's happening with him now? His behaviour has suddenly changed?' and the doctor didn't know. He couldn't give me an answer and he couldn't advise me what to do." Understanding challenging behaviour is the most difficult part of dementia caregiving because, as mentioned earlier, the disease is unique to each person and each one reacts differently. It would make an enormous difference to caregivers if Dr Brunet's plan of having a dementia nurse in each surgery were taken up: someone with training and an understanding of different dementia patterns.

The Prime Minister acknowledged the need for emotional and psychological support for caregivers when he said that councils would be required, by law, to offer it to dementia caregivers, along with practical help and respite care. Sadly, there was no mention of any money to fund it, and councils are already bracing themselves for a huge reduction in their social care budgets as part of austerity measures. Although it's widely understood that dementia caregiver burden is subjective, this was the first time I've seen this kind of need publicly mentioned. In this chapter, along with practical pointers, there are little pathways that caregivers can take to guard their hearts.

Circles of support

When you are caring for someone with dementia, you are the key person in their life, the hub at the centre of the wheel. You juggle their healthcare, their social life, their finances; in fact, everything. At times you may feel as if you are carrying the world on your shoulders, so it makes sense to have a sound practical, as well as a spiritual, foundation. Being "practical" means looking at all our resources and, not surprisingly, our biggest resource in times of need, after God Himself, is His people.

Like Ezekiel's "wheels within wheels", throughout our lives most of us have circles of people who support us in different ways. They give us momentum, encouragement, and direction. They overlap and change over time and circumstances, having greater or lesser significance. We tend to take them for granted until we really need them, but when dementia enters your life, you need to identify your circles of support and make sure that they are firmly in place for you and, hopefully, overlapping in places and working together. Now is not the time to let events roll over you. Now is the time to engage with people, and make sure that they are available.

Not everyone is good at "engaging" with people. "It's all very well if you're that sort of person," someone told me. It came up because her doctor's surgery seems to be overwhelmed at times, and it was quite a common sight to see patients line up outside from 7.00 in the morning, hoping for an appointment. That didn't work very well and didn't look good to passers-by, either, so it was changed to an appointment-by-telephone system, and patients were told to ring between 6.30 and 8.15 each morning to make an appointment. Unfortunately, this patient found the lines continually engaged.

"I tried sixty times," she said.

I suggested, "Why don't you send the head doctor a humorous little card, marked 'Personal', with a little note inside saying, 'Help! How can I arrange to see you? I keep phoning but can't get through!"

She was aghast. "*You* might do that, but I couldn't – I'm not that sort of person!" she said.

Being able to engage with people is often hampered by a lack of assertiveness. Being assertive is not the same thing as being aggressive. It's simply being able to say what needs to be said. It's about respecting your own feelings, and standing up for them without shaming or humiliating the other person. It helps to use "I" statements rather than "you"; being collaborative rather than accusing. For example, saying, "It's important to me that promises be kept" instead of "You should keep your promise", and "This is how it looks to me" instead of "This is how you are!"

People lack assertiveness for all sorts of reasons – for fear they will receive a negative, hurtful response, or that they won't be listened to: that, in effect, they'll be rejected. Suzanne was seething with frustration because she hadn't been able to tell her boss how she felt about a programme their department was running. She rarely felt able to tell him anything that was not superficial, yet she was an intelligent, efficient woman. We rehearsed what she would say several times, until she felt comfortable with actually saying the words. The following week she did speak to him and he listened with such respect that it totally changed her attitude to being assertive. (It also helped to change her attitude about herself.) So check your assertiveness. If necessary, rehearse what you need to say in front of a mirror. Because, as sure as God made little green apples, you're going to need it on this journey. You're going to be dealing with consultants, doctors, nurses, social workers, and domiciliary carers, as well as friends and family. You can do it! I've seen quiet women become warriors when their children were threatened. In fact, several women have told me that they only learned how to be assertive when they had to go to their children's school or speak to other parents with a concern.

The circle of family

Looking at your circles of support, you'll see that your first one is your immediate family. If possible, have a get-together and let them know that you, and their loved one, are going to need them. Ask them to make regular visits. So many caregivers tell us about relatives who stay away because they can't cope with the emotional demands. Remind them that the person remains, even though their behaviour will change in response to the brain damage. Arrange for them to come and sit, so you can have a break. A lady in my fellowship said that simply being able to come to a church meeting because a relative took over was such a blessing; it just helped her to feel she could carry on. Perhaps one relative is good with the internet, and can be on hand to help find information, or fill in online forms. Another could help with the shopping, or the laundry. I met two sisters living near each other who shared the care of their father, who was doubly incontinent and very poorly. They couldn't have done it without the full support of their husbands.

Their arrangements were that he lived for three weeks in one home, and three weeks in another, and while in one home the other sister would come and collect the laundry. The difference it made to them, simply being there for each other, was immeasurable. Doing the laundry was much more than a practical help – it was saying, "I know how much you have to do and I want to lift this part off you."

Empathy, emotional support, encouragement, and practical help are all things that families can provide – even if they need to be reminded, and, sadly, many relatives *do* need to be reminded. Hazel and Tom were looking after Tom's father and at the start his brothers and sister were a great support, visiting regularly. But, as Dad deteriorated, their visits became fewer and fewer and then petered out altogether. It was because they couldn't cope with Dad's behaviour and oddness, they said. It upset them. And they were so busy with their own lives. If you have a family member looking after a loved one with dementia, don't stay away. You don't have to do the laundry, but there are other things you could do.

The circle of friends

"A true friend sticks closer than a brother," says Proverbs 18:24, and sometimes friends are closer than natural family. You will be sharing a zillion things with them, as one does, even before the journey officially begins. Find a moment to tell them that it's important that they keep visiting and telephoning, and making sure that you don't slide into isolation. Many friends will be part of your church fellowship – tell them you need encouragement from the Scriptures, and to know that they'll be praying for you.

If you're caring for a parent or other elderly relative, remember their friends, too. You may need to explain that although your mother or father will change as the disease progresses, they are still the same person inside and they will be blessed by friends who visit. Explain that even though Mum may forget who they are, she will still feel the emotional warmth that exists between them. Our cognitive memories may be lost with dementia, but our emotional memories stay with us for ever. One of the hurtful things Jean remembers is her mother's friends saying that she wasn't the same person any more because she wasn't responding to them as she used to; she couldn't remember all the times they'd spent together and she wasn't her old sparky self, and after a while they stopped visiting. Jean hadn't had the opportunity to tell them that even though her mother had changed in their eyes she was still the same person, and still needed the warmth of their friendship.

The circle of church

Many people have told us how they slipped off the church radar screen and felt abandoned, but that seems to be changing now. We are hearing from many churches who really do want to help, and most of them already are. Many now have dementia champions and are looking to become completely dementia-friendly. When the illness goes on for years, others, including family, friends, and church fellowships, tend to think that this is just their life now; this is how it is. There's also the tendency of our society to force into isolation people who are under pressure, said Kitwood.[1] "No individual was ever designed for such an onerous commitment," he wrote. "Even in those rare situations where the care is genuinely shared by several members of the family, the situation is far less fraught and strained."

People in your fellowship can assure you that you will not be forgotten when the illness keeps you away, that you will be prayed for, and that there will be someone to make sure you are encouraged and supported spiritually. There are simple ways of "befriending", including making sure you get "church news" regularly. There may be someone who can be telephoned in a crisis, or when you feel in need of prayer. Dementia champions in churches can make the world of difference. They can organize a team of willing people with different talents who can spare different amounts of time; they just need to be given the opportunity. You can ask your pastor or dementia champion to visit so you can talk about the things that you might need. Even the smallest touch can make a vast difference. A wife told how blessed she was when the vicar said to her that he was amazed that she could get to church at all, and that it was good to see her. Often, it's simply knowing that people at church are willing to help, and are on call. But it's important that the church doesn't allow you to slowly drop out of sight.

The circle of medical and helping professionals

Everything here is more complex than it used to be. Where there used to be just your GP and a practice nurse, there are now multi-disciplinary teams (MDT) bringing different specialisms, including an occupational therapist and a nurse. Hospital consultants seem to have been pushed higher up the "accessibility" pyramid than ever, possibly because there are not enough of them. When it comes to assessment of needs, *your* needs should be examined as well as those of the person you are caring for. They'll probably give you informative literature but you can expect much more than that. They should have a sympathetic, listening manner, and be able to give you a clear explanation of the disease, and an idea of what to expect as it develops. They'll know what medication is available, and should be able to refer you to other sources of help.

If the teams work as they are predicted to, they'll also be able to tell you how to obtain specialist advice when there are changes or things you are concerned about. Sometimes people with dementia develop other diseases. A daughter whose father also developed cancer told us that over a three-year period she spoke to over thirty different doctors, nurses, other health workers, and social workers, each one asking the same questions, looking for the same information, but with an emphasis on different aspects. Recently there was a press story about an eighty-six-year-old who was admitted to a hospital ward after going through the A&E unit. The admitting nurse on the hospital ward asked for the same information her daughter had already given in A&E. To make it worse, this nurse had turned her back on the old lady to face her computer, and shouted the questions over her shoulder as she completed the form on the screen. It will help if you put all the details you know will be needed on a piece of paper and make lots of photocopies. That way, you can simply hand the information over. There will probably still be questions, but, all being well, far fewer.

The circle of God

The most important circle around you is God Himself: "As the mountains surround Jerusalem, so the Lord surrounds His people from this time forth and forever" Psalm 125:2 (NKJV). He promises to strengthen us at tough times in our pilgrimage. It isn't just pie-in-the-sky, fluffy thinking – He does what He says he will. Many Christians talk about this "surrounding", of sensing the presence of God. While she was battling cancer, Barbara Johnson, author of *Laughter from Heaven*, wrote, "Here I am, still battling cancer, still sporting a hairstyle more appropriate for a marine than a grandmother, my front tooth out and my wig two rooms away, and yet I have an overwhelming feeling that all is well. As ridiculous as it might be to someone else, I feel like I'm in heaven on earth."[2]

One of the most extraordinary examples of God's "surrounding" is described by Canon Andrew White, Emeritus Vicar of St George's Church, Baghdad. His book *Faith under Fire* is one of the most powerful and faith-building books I have ever read. We've heard of the horrors perpetrated by the extremists in Iraq. Andrew has seen so much brokenness and tragedy there, on such a scale that he can't bring himself to describe it fully in writing. He speaks wherever he can about the suffering that he and the people of St George's Church go through. Some of the things are so unspeakable that he has learned not to describe them in any kind of detail because it is too much for the average person to bear. He states simply and powerfully that, in the middle of the horror, he is filled with joy. "We are an Easter people," he writes. "Like all Easter people, our symbol is the cross – a symbol of death but also a symbol of hope, of life and of resurrection. That which represents a cruel, violent death also represents new and eternal life."[3] *Faith under Fire* is a book that will encourage you, in the real sense of the word, in all your circumstances. "It will do your heart good," as an older Christian used to say when recommending something to me.

How to do your heart good

"Is it possible to train someone with dementia into more acceptable behaviour?" was a question we were asked at the end of a conference. I was amazed, because three speakers had shown from several different perspectives that when someone has dementia they've lost cognitive capacity; they're not able to hold in their minds a sequence of thoughts leading to actions. They have a functional memory deficit. But what the questioners, a couple looking after mother-in-law, were really looking for was a way of *modifying* difficult behaviour, and training was just an idea they were putting forward. Their underlying problem was that the person they were looking after had always been manipulative and they believed that her behaviour, now that she had dementia, was simply more of the same. There's an incredible tension in having to care for someone you believe is trying to control you. But manipulating a situation means being able to hold in your head more than one idea and neatly joining the dots, along the lines of "If I do this then this will happen and this is what it will mean to them…" and people with dementia aren't able to reason like that. Sometimes, too, it helps to know that people who tend to be manipulative and controlling feel vulnerable and fear rejection: they have to manipulate events in order to be included in them. It can be tough looking after someone with difficult traits, especially as dementia sometimes exaggerates them, so it helps to know that, whatever the person is doing, if they have dementia they're not doing it deliberately.

It's also a time for accepting what you can't change, and for recognizing that in caring for the person you are acting in line with your values. It reaffirms your integrity. If you're a Christian, those values will include service and self-sacrifice, allowing a grinding of your soul to shape you into becoming more like Jesus. But He won't leave you to bear it on your own. "I can do all things through Christ who strengthens me" (Philippians 4:13) is a favourite verse for many, but to my mind Psalm 18:29 is more robust, with action in it: "For by You I can run upon a troop; And by my God I can leap over a wall (KJV)." Often the walls we have to leap over are those within our souls, negative beliefs erected brick by brick over a lifetime.

There's also a way of deliberately choosing thoughts that will help. It sounds hippy and zany, but it really works. It's called "compassionate thinking", and research has found that it has positive effects on the immune system and helps the brain's "soothing" response. Some years ago a study of a group of CompuServe employees in America produced some interesting results. A group of employees practised compassionate meditation for six weeks. Another group practised thinking negative thoughts, and those on the waiting list were a control group. At the end of six weeks, researchers found that the compassionate thinking group had increased positive emotions, mindfulness, and feelings of purpose in life and social support, and decreased symptoms of illness. There were no changes in the waiting list control group, and the "negative thinking" group were not a happy bunch at all.

It's a scriptural precept, of course, to practise "loving kindness". We do it when we pray, because it's not possible to pray without compassion. If you are caring for someone with dementia whose behaviour is troubling you, you could try compassionate thinking. Write down loving thoughts about yourself and, separately, about the person, and read them for about ten minutes – or just five minutes if time is short, once a day. Or just deliberately think kind thoughts. Our brains incline instinctively towards the negative, so for most of us it takes more practice than we anticipate simply to think kind thoughts, especially about ourselves. Ask someone to tell you ten negative things about themselves and they will do it in a flash, but ask for ten positive attributes and they really have to think hard about it, so you may need to write down your kindly thoughts about yourself.

There is also a growing interest in "mindfulness", and it is being introduced into some schools, I read, with good results. Mindfulness is said to be "a mental state achieved by focusing one's awareness on the present moment, while calmly acknowledging and accepting one's feelings, thoughts, and bodily sensations, used as a therapeutic technique". The aim is to still the mind until one is totally in the present moment; not ruminating or stressing in the river of thoughts that normally run through it. Recent studies by researchers at Massachusetts General Hospital and Harvard Medical School show that "certain regions of the brain respond to mindfulness meditation by reorganising their structure, an example of the phenomenon known as neuroplasticity".[4] At a lecture at the University of South Wales, Professor Mark Williams, author of a book on mindfulness,[5] included scans, graphs, and diagrams showing its positive effects on brain structure as well as on the mind.

But, despite an article in the Association of Christian Counsellors' magazine *Accord*, I have a couple of reservations about it. The first is that it has its roots in Buddhist practice, though set against that is that we know that every good thing comes from God (James 1:17), and the other is that nowhere in the Bible are we told to empty our minds of our thoughts but, rather, to be selective about what we choose to take in and dwell on (Philippians 4:8). We're also told to subject every thought to Christ's scrutiny (2 Corinthians 10:5). An empty mind also seems to be an invitation to invasion. "Be clear-minded and alert. Your opponent, the devil, is prowling around like a roaring lion, looking for someone to devour," Peter told his flock (1 Peter 5:8, ISV). We live in such a materialistic world that it is easy to forget that it is also inhabited by invisible entities that are at war with us – which is why there is a helmet in the set of spiritual armour described in Ephesians 6:11–18. Our battle is a spiritual one, particularly the battle of the mind.

Meditation is part of Christian life, and there is a mindfulness practice in which we can still our minds and bring our thoughts captive to Christ. Some people suffering from stress have unwelcome thoughts that race around their minds like Exocet missiles. In contrast, with depression, thoughts can be so heavy that they won't move on, won't go away. So I devised Christian Mindfulness. Jim, whose mind leaped from one thought to another so fast that I wondered if it would ever slow to "normal", tried it. He recorded the directions on his phone with suitable timings in between, and practised it twice a day. After a couple of weeks he said it helped him so much that it was sometimes the only thing that got him to work in the morning. Ralph, whose thoughts were depressed and slow, practised it in counselling. He said that he felt filled with fresh air and joy. A copy of it is at the back of the book, in Appendix 1.

But, if all you have is a few minutes, practise breathing properly. When you breathe in, your diaphragm should move out, and when you breathe out it should move in. Babies and children do it naturally, but we seem to forget. Try sitting in a comfortable position, in a quiet place: breathe in deeply, and breathe out slowly. (Put your hand on your waist to check that you're breathing in and out properly.) At the same time say in your mind, "Jesus, I am breathing in your Holy Spirit" and "Lord, I am breathing out these thoughts to You". In a tense situation, including when you are standing or walking, you can go to your "breathing centre" and do the same thing. A lady in her eighties was grieved and stressed by her husband's behaviour, and had started to have irregular heartbeats, she said, so we practised "focused breathing". We met at a conference three years later and she told me how much the breathing practice had helped her.

If you're a caregiver it's very important that you take little "pleasure" breaks during the day. A commercial on TV showed a mother opening the door to a babysitter and showing her into the room with the baby before going into the kitchen to make herself a cup of hot chocolate. She took the cup of hot chocolate into a room by herself, sat in a big comfortable chair, and savoured it with a sense of deep self-indulgence. We all need "hot-chocolate moments", though they may be reading a book, listening to music, cooking, calling a friend on the phone – there's an endless variety. Often I'll stop what I'm doing during the day and listen to a worship song on YouTube.

You can also take some spiritual "medication". It is a good idea to write out some verses on Post-it® notes and stick them where you are likely to see them, such as on the bathroom mirror, inside a wardrobe or a cupboard door, and somewhere in the kitchen. Good examples are: 1 John 1:7, Psalm 138:8, Proverbs 8:10, Romans 8:38–39, Luke 1:37, Philippians 4:6, Philippians 4:13, and 2 Corinthians 9:8. A number of scripture verses are given in Appendix 2. The Scriptures are "active and living" (Hebrews 4:12), and penetrate precisely to the heart of the matter. Christians have based their lives on the truth revealed in the Bible. It is not like any other book: it is God's word, and He watches over it to perform it (Jeremiah 1:12).

Frustration and guilt, stress and grief form the biggest share of dementia caregiver burden. A Welsh pastor told of storming out of the room in sheer frustration after his mother had asked for the umpteenth time if there was a meeting that evening. The minute he closed the door he was filled with guilt, telling himself that here he was, a pastor preaching Christian virtues, behaving like this with his mother, who he knew loved him dearly. Then the Lord reminded him that "the blood of Jesus his Son cleanses us from all sin" (1 John 1:7, ESV).

I can't think of a single caregiver who has not known frustration. One of the most wearing and frustrating things that George had to do was to persuade his wife, over and over again, that she wasn't a burden, that he wasn't planning to leave her, and that she was not worthless. Frustration is a normal emotional response to many of the difficulties of being a dementia caregiver. Guilt is what we feel when we fall short of our values, including having unkind thoughts, and we can even feel guilty about feeling guilty. Thank God that we know, like the Welsh preacher, about Jesus.

Perhaps the two biggest dangers to emotional well-being are stress and grief. Prolonged or intense stress can make caregivers physically or verbally aggressive. The warning signs that you are approaching a crisis are having a knot in the throat, feeling short of breath, having stomach cramps or chest pains or a headache, and – ominously – a desire to strike out. If it's too intense, leave the room for a moment and practise focused "Holy Spirit" breathing.

Our feelings do not take God by surprise. And He knows we need to call on Him for help all the time – He even encouraged it when he told us about the widow and the unrighteous judge

(Luke 18:1–8). "As for me, I will call upon God; and the Lord shall save me. Evening, and morning, and at noon, will I pray, and cry aloud: and he shall hear my voice," says Psalm 55:16–17 (KJV). It's worth saying again that the Lord Jesus Christ takes your caregiving very personally. He is on record as saying, "I tell you all with certainty, since you did it for one of the least important of these brothers of mine, you did it for me" (Matthew 25:40, ISV).

Many experts believe that the most debilitating emotion suffered by dementia caregivers is grief. Grief is said to be living with absence, and losing a loved one with dementia is an absence that grows more and more over time. There is grief for the loss of the person they knew intimately, for the loss of a future together, for the loss of relationship and, on top of that, grief for the losses the dementia sufferer is experiencing. Often caregivers' grief is not recognized by others, including medical professionals. It's just not taken into account, even by those who are trying to help them. When a crisis becomes chronic, without realizing it people can feel that "it's just their life; that's how it is…" So their grief becomes disenfranchised, unacknowledged by those around them. It can be even more complicated after bereavement, because the first step in a grieving process is to acknowledge the loss, and then express emotion. A friend who lost his wife to cancer soon after they'd married used to come and sit over cups of tea, just going over and over the same things – how she'd died, how he couldn't see life ahead without her, how he couldn't bear to move her clothes or any of her belongings, how he was feeling… People deal with grief in different ways but we do need others to acknowledge our loss.

Most of us, especially if we're British, find it hard to articulate our deepest emotions, or know how to help others with theirs. There's still a legacy of the stiff upper lip about us, despite the influence of thousands of immigrants from more expressive nations. Fortunately, there's another way – of just being there, alongside, like Job's friends. And I think it's very important to remind people who are in this dark valley of grief that they need to look after themselves.

One of the hardest things is consoling people who don't know Jesus. He knows about grief. The description of his emotions in Isaiah 53:3 is almost unbearable. Yet for the Christian there is the hope that we have in Jesus Christ, and the knowledge that we are pilgrims here, journeying to a destination that is so wonderful that the Bible says we can't even imagine it. "No eye has seen, no ear has heard, and no mind has imagined what God has prepared for those who love him" (1 Corinthians 2:9, NLT). "Until then, we do grieve, but not as those without hope" (1 Thessalonians 4:13).

Finally, although it sounds counter-intuitive, whatever your role in life right now, look for the joy in day-to-day activities, the things you can take pleasure in and the things to thank God for, including those "hot-chocolate moments". If you are a caregiver, think of the positive aspects of what you are doing, and how it all contributes to your loved one's well-being. Remember God's promises, and think forward to the moment when you will hear the Lord say, "Well done, good and faithful servant! You have been faithful with a few things: I will put you in charge of many things. Come and share your master's happiness" (Matthew 25:23, NIV).

Notes

1. Kitwood, *Dementia Reconsidered*.
2. Barbara Johnson *Laughter from Heaven*, Nashville, TN: W Publishing Group, 2004.
3. Andrew White, *Faith under Fire: What the Middle East Conflict Has Taught Me about God*, Oxford: Monarch Books, 2011.
4. Jon Kabat-Zinn, *Full Catastrophe Living*, London: Piatkus, revised edition 2013.
5. Mark Williams and Danny Penman *Mindfulness: A Practical Guide to Finding Peace in a Frantic World*, London: Piatkus, 2011.

Chapter 10
When Hope Shines Through

God keeps His word

... and hope does not disappoint, because the love of
God has been poured out within our hearts through the
Holy Spirit who was given to us. (Romans 5:5, NASB)

I'm not sure whether other languages have a version of the saying "The proof of the pudding is in the eating", but when we put together different ingredients for brain-boosting sessions for older people in one of our housing complexes, that's exactly what we were looking for – proof that people working together in a group, receiving mental and spiritual stimulation, would achieve positive results. We came up with a concept, chose the ingredients, mixed them all together, and tried them out, and the results were better than we had imagined. The thing we hadn't expected, but which proved to be the most beneficial of all for those involved, was the sense of close community and of belonging that developed among the participants.

More and more studies were confirming the plasticity of the brain and how it responds to stimuli, so we (Janet and I) wondered what the results would be if we mixed together some cognitive stimulation with spiritual support, self-affirmation and sense of achievement with fellowship and fun, and put them into a format with changing content that could be repeated as part of a series. An important premise was that participants would be working together. In our plan we wrote, "Aims: a) cognitive stimulation: reinforce and affirm individual identity, especially in Christ; b) increase sociability; c) provide sense of achievement; d) boost spiritual awareness (thankfulness, worship, connectedness); and e) enjoy companionship and engagement and have fun."

We called the series "Brain and Soul Boosting for Seniors", and tried it initially with people living independently in the housing complex. The self-affirmation element was particularly important because, as they become frailer, older people sometimes feel "less than", and their sense of worth diminishes. As people with dementia become more and more affected by failing memory, they too benefit by having their sense of identity and value confirmed.

Janet's entire career has been spent caring for older people, first as a psychogeriatric nurse and then in managing care homes. She has a natural affinity with older people and a reassuring, soothing manner, and if ever I become old and frail I'll ask the Lord to send me an identikit Janet. So, after the sessions had been themed and we'd decided what outcomes we'd like to see, we put the idea to the managers in the housing complex. We thought it would appeal to occupants who would like to keep their brains sharp, but the care manager, Georgina, encouraged a group of people who had early dementia to try it, and that's how it started. Sometimes there were six people, sometimes eight, and occasionally ten, but because the approach is very "person-centred", Janet found the ideal number was eight. They came with different backgrounds, abilities, and interests; they included a minister and a pastor, a music teacher, an architect, and an art teacher. Some had difficulty in speaking, a couple had severe memory impairment, one person had mild cognitive impairment, and so on, but they brought themselves and a willingness to engage with Janet and each other. One lady in particular was always anxious when she arrived, wringing her hands and sometimes very hesitant about coming in, but by the end of each session she was always smiling and happy and less anxious.

The "proof of the pudding" was better than we'd thought. After a couple of months participants had become a friendship group, sitting with each other at mealtimes in the dining room, and helping each other in different ways. Janet remembers that the two with the severest impairments, who had difficulty speaking, became especially firm friends. They were all far less anxious and had improved memories, finding it easier to make their way back to their apartments, and some, said Georgina, would not need reminding of the day that the meeting was held – they remembered. She noticed, too, that the change in the "dementia group" had affected everyone else living there.

She said, "The dread of dementia is dead here. The atmosphere is totally transformed. Others feel more confident about helping people (in the group); for instance, they'll turn them round if they see they're going the wrong way, and they're sitting behind them at devotions and handing them the hymn book at the right place."

Janet recalls some outstanding moments. Walter, who rarely spoke because he had trouble with words, volunteered to close with prayer, and it was such a lovely prayer that everyone looked to him to close each session after that. And Janet especially remembers the session on "Avocado – hailed as the new anti-ageing superfood".

She recalls, "We discussed the item and decided we need a variety of foods to be healthy, which is more important than fad diets and 'in' foods. During the warm-up quiz, one of the ladies, who has difficulty with reasoning and with recalling memories, surprised us by voluntarily offering an answer. I had asked for the names of food categories and we wrote them on the flip chart, and she said 'Apples and bananas', and after obviously trying to contribute more, said, 'Are they fruits?' This is the first time she has contributed since we started the sessions. When I have asked for her input and tried to draw her into contributing she has always said, 'I am sorry I can't remember'. It was a wonderful moment.

"The activity where pictures of food and their country of origin had to be matched went down very well. Two were easy, two they had to think about and needed a couple of clues, two were more difficult and they mismatched them. I was pleased it seemed to be at the right level for this group.

"One gentleman appeared to be asleep during the session, only rousing momentarily when prompted. (I felt he looked rather unwell.) However, at the end of the session, I asked if anyone would like to pray and he immediately started to pray. After having a cup of tea together I was escorting him to the door when he looked at me and said he had vitamin B12 every three months! As we had been looking at the pictures of foods mentioned in the Bible I had talked briefly about lamb being good for providing vitamins B3 and B12. It was obvious that some of the session had registered with him even though he had not participated! This blessed me so much. It was a great session and they said they had enjoyed it and would come again. This is a breakthrough, as two of the ladies have been reluctant to attend but both said how good it had been and they would be coming next week."

On one occasion, in the middle of a session Sheila was called out by her GP practice nurse who wanted to take a blood test. It was in the middle of an interesting discussion and Sheila didn't want to miss a thing, so she insisted the nurse take the blood sample in the corridor outside so she could continue to watch what was happening through the glass door. Apathy and lethargy are twin hazards of old age, so to raise this level of interest is unusual. Janet was particularly blessed when, several months later, as she passed by the big lounge, she spotted Walter, whose dementia had worsened, and smiled at him. His eyes lit as he obviously remembered her. Another resident noticed how glad he was to see her.

We are planning to publish the "Brain and Soul Boosting" sessions and make them available for churches for their older folk, and for those in their local community. Our experience shows that they work at two levels – for older people who may have mild cognitive impairment, and for those with early–mid-stage dementia, bearing in mind that each person is different at each stage.

* * *

When good care is a path to miracles

Three of us were sitting in a large, bright room, with the sun outside lighting up the elegant landscaped garden. On the windowsill is an attractive display of paintings and photographs, and, standing a few feet in front, slightly at an angle, is an artist's easel holding a painting in progress. The only sign on the door is the name of the person who lives here, but there should be another, declaring "Artist in residence". We are in a Pilgrims' nursing home in Leicester, which is now the home of seventy-five-year-old Tony, a former book illustrator and art teacher, who has Lewy body dementia. It took eight years of struggle to get a diagnosis.

Tony's wife, Sue, says they saw "geriatric psychiatrists, a neuropsychologist, an occupational therapist and a social worker, geriatricians by the tonne, psychogeriatrians (who all seemed to need counselling themselves), a sleep apnoea specialist, and a community psychiatric nurse" before they saw a neurologist and paid privately for a SPECT scan, which revealed the Lewy bodies in his brain. At one stage, she recalls, "As we were sitting together, holding hands, we were told that it could be caused by marital problems, and were advised to go to Relate."

With the diagnosis Sue was told that Tony had only a few months to live, and was advised to find a good nursing home. "He was dying. He was doubly incontinent, in a wheelchair, and had been given three months to live. That was five years ago," she said.

Now, as we were speaking (five years later), Tony has improved so much that Sue says people think she is making it up when she tells them about the "before" and the "now".

"He'd stopped painting, but he's an artist; all these are Tony's works," she says, waving a hand around his room. The pictures include some of his book illustrations and the "Ladybird" books' covers.

Tony nodded and said, "That's the sort of work I did. I am more at ease with illustrations."

The most beautiful picture in the room is a photograph taken at his daughter's wedding some eighteen months earlier. They are smiling with delight into each other's eyes, Lucy a radiant bride and Tony a handsome father. Yet it was an event that no one thought he would be able to attend.

"Lucy didn't expect him there at all," Sue said. "Only they said in here, let's go for it; let's try it. It wasn't local, it was in York, and I'd obviously gone to try and sort things out. I couldn't get him dressed – carers had to do it here. One of the staff came in extra early and then discovered that his shirt wouldn't button so they had to move the buttons. "

"I honestly couldn't wish for anything better than I'm getting here," Tony told me. "All the staff… they're so attentive. They go out of their way; if they can do anything, they'll stop what they're doing." It's been an exceptionally tough journey for Sue. She has some advice for people struggling to get a diagnosis. "Keep a diary. Make it a big diary with a day to view, and write everything significant in it. When you see the doctor or the consultant, take it with you.

"And find someone who will listen to you. Search until you find one person. You can't measure empathy – it's priceless. You need to be able to say, 'My husband doesn't fit the clinical description. I love my husband and something's gone wrong with his head." Sue's person was a community psychiatric nurse (CPN), who used to come to the house.

She remembers, "The CPN had a long case list of similarly affected men, whose wives were climbing up the wall trying to get someone to listen to their odd stories of aberrant behaviour and personality change." Tony's diagnosis prompted the CPN to check all her other undiagnosed patients with similar symptoms, enabling her to ask neurologists and geriatricians and other specialists to check these people for LBD. It's a small consolation to Sue that Tony's illness has helped others, but it is a comfort, nevertheless. She's now very involved in the Lewy Body Dementia Society, and continually researches into the condition, finding out what is working for people with Lewy body dementia. Combining that knowledge with "the wonderful care here" [in the home] enhances his well-being, she says, adding, "Obviously the prime mover in that is the power of the Lord, and I am sure that without prayer he would not be alive today. And there's this daily role of prayerfulness and singing in Tony's life these days. As he becomes increasingly frail and when Lewy takes a hold (which can be any time of the day or night), staying inside ('confined to barracks', Tony calls it, from army days in India!) enables us to be more involved in the family life of the home… sharing morning or afternoon prayer, services, Communion. It's at these times that I feel I can be of help with other residents, some of whom rarely have visitors. Also, in talking to other carers I get strength and wisdom and faith (I love in particular talking to Paul Clarke, who is a truly special man and pastor), and I learn about patience. It helps me so much when I feel alone and Tony takes an emotional sabbatical from me." Paul Clarke is a pastor whose wife Lillian also had Lewy Body dementia and was in the same care home. Paul became pastor to others while Lillian was in the home. He was very valued by residents and staff.

* * *

When God turns it for good

"And we know that all that happens to us is working for our good if we love God and are fitting into his plans," Paul says in his letter to the Christians living in Rome (Romans 8:28, MSG). But we usually don't see this until *after* the difficult circumstances, when the trying times are over. And it may be months or even years before we see it. But I saw it in one of the most trying caregiving situations I'd ever heard of. When I met Zoë at a national conference, she had about her an air of resignation, of despair almost. She'd been caring for her mother for about a year, and although she was clearly a competent person who had known to involve Social Services from the outset and pull in as much help as was available, she looked much burdened.

The complicating factors were her family, and her own quiet, retiring nature. She had a big family, mostly still living in England, but they had "deserted" her and her mother and had dropped completely out of touch. For various reasons it had been necessary to move both parents into her house so she could care for her mother, but her father had long had mental health problems and didn't believe that his wife had dementia. He not only opposed any kind of care but, when he thought Zoë was out of earshot, he would take hold of his wife's upper arms and shake her, telling her to pull herself together. It was a tremendous strain for Zoë, trying to care for her mother and help her father at the same time, and it called for continual hypervigilance on her part. Zoë was the youngest of seven children, and seemed to have "tag-end" syndrome: as she'd grown up she'd rarely been listened to or been given much attention. It's not always the case with large families; in fact, sometimes it's the opposite, and the youngest is coddled with love and protection by older siblings. Often it depends on the love and time parents give each one. For Zoë, having a father with mental health problems and a mother who seemed distant and withdrawn meant learning to keep herself to herself, expecting not to be heard, and becoming "a loner", as she put it.

Zoë loved the Lord, however, and had come to the national event with a group from her church. But they didn't know about her situation, because she hadn't thought to tell them.

"Is that fair to them?" I asked. "How can they pray and how can they help if they don't know?" She said she'd think about it. As for the absent siblings, had she asked them why they'd stopped coming to visit their mother? No, she hadn't thought of doing that, but she would send them an email. My heart went out to this quiet, courageous lady. When I saw her a couple of days later she looked different, so much more relaxed and upbeat at the same time. Discounting the fact that this happens to everyone at this particular event, where the worship each day is wonderful and a big marquee is set aside with a music group playing all day so you can go and sit and simply worship at any time of the day, it was still evident that there'd been a major shift in Zoë. After we'd spoken the day before she had shared what was happening with her church members, who seemed to have simply flowed around her like water around a rock, with everyone asking how they could help and how they could pray. I felt it was a major breakthrough for Zoë. Then we met several months later in a different context, and she told me how she'd emailed her family and they'd replied, saying, in so many words, that they didn't know what to say or how to simply be with their mother. But they agreed to visit, and they kept their word.

The best thing of all was that, as the dementia took hold, her mother began to share more of her own childhood, which helped Zoë understand a lot about her. For the first time in her life, Zoë was able to spend "quality" time with her mother, and they got to know each other at a level that they'd never been able to before. Zoë said, "I even had hugs! I'd never had hugs before."

So out of this terribly difficult situation came three life-changing discoveries. In showing their love and willingness to be involved, her church showed Zoë that they valued her, and cared for her. She learned that coming out of her corner had good results – she was strengthened for many other "comings out", too. Gently challenging her siblings told her that the reason they didn't come wasn't that they didn't care, but that they didn't know what to do, and her taking the initiative reopened healthy lines of communication. And, best of all, God released to Zoë the mother's love that she'd not known when she was a child.

Jesus always has time for you

When times are tough it's so easy to believe that God has taken His eye off us, that Jesus is tied up with more important things. But there's an account in the Bible of when Jesus interrupted the most important journey in the history of the universe to comfort one person. The story, in John's Gospel (20:11–18), tells us that after His resurrection He stopped outside the tomb to speak to a grieving Mary Magdalene. Mary was there all by herself. I believe that it wasn't just her grief that was troubling her so, but the feeling that all of reasonable life had ended for her; even, perhaps, that the demons He had cast out would return. She had made Jesus the centre, the rock of her life, and now not only had He been murdered, but His body stolen. All trace of Him had gone from her life.

Jesus was on His way to present His resurrection body to His Father God, to put the full stop to the sentence that was written before time began, which would usurp Satan's claim to the earth and restore to it the ownership and authority of heaven. He was the sacrificial lamb and the priest, "holy, harmless, undefiled, separate from sinners, and made higher than the heavens" (Hebrews 7:26, KJV), and this presentation to the Father would reverberate throughout all eternity. Yet He paused on this momentous journey for Mary.

"Don't touch me," He cautioned, "for I haven't yet ascended to the Father. But go find my brothers and tell them that I ascend to my Father and your Father, my God and your God." Some commentators say that He was warning Mary not to cling to Him, not to hold Him back, and others point to the commandment in Haggai 2:13 about the rules when presenting the sacrificial blood of atonement. He was preparing to enter the heavenly temple with His own blood to obtain eternal redemption for us. But, whichever way you look at it, whatever the reason, the fact is that He paused to speak to a woman with a broken heart.

Every story in the Bible is there for a reason. I believe that this one is the pathway to one of the greatest hopes – that Jesus will meet us at the point of deepest need, even in dementia, when all trace of Him seems to have gone from our world.

* * *

As the rain hides the stars,
As the autumn mist hides the hills,
As the clouds veil the blue of the sky,
So the dark happenings of my lot
Hide the shining of your face from me.
Yet, if I may hold Your hand
In the darkness, it is enough,
Since I know that
though I may stumble in my going,
You do not fail.[1]

Notes

1. From *Celtic Prayers of Yesterday and Today*, Oxford: Lion Hudson, 1996.

Appendix 1

Research shows that practising mindfulness has beneficial effects on the brain, the immune system, and individuals' sense of well-being. For Christians, it is important that all we do should be acceptable to God, and under His wing. We are to guard our hearts and our minds (Ephesians 5).

This meditation/mindfulness session can take between ten and thirty minutes. It's best if you record the directions, perhaps on your mobile phone, leaving space, to suit you, between each step.

Christian Mindfulness

Sit straight in an upright chair with your back firmly against the back of the chair, hands resting on the tops of your legs.

- Commit this time, and your mind, body, and spirit, to the Lord Jesus Christ.

- Lower your eyelids, or close your eyes, whichever is more comfortable for you.

- Sit upright, with your back against the back of the chair.

- Focus your attention on your body. Concentrate, one by one, for a few moments on your feet; then your ankles, your shins, and your knees. Feel their warmth, and weight, one by one.

- Feel your back firmly against the chair, then your shoulders, your neck and your head. Notice the warmth, and the weight.

- Then come to your centre – your breathing. Just observe how you are breathing; don't control it. Notice how it happens all by itself. Focus on your diaphragm – the area of your breathing. Focus on your breath.

- If thoughts intrude, bring them to your "breathing centre" and gently breathe them out.

- Visualize the Holy Spirit at the centre of your being. (John 15:26). He is our breath of life. Visualize breathing him in, and, as you breathe out, breathing out negative thoughts.

- Envisage breathing out negativity, and breathing in the Breath of Life.

- After a few minutes, switch from focusing to "monitoring". Think of your mind as a vast open sky and your thoughts, feelings, and sensations as passing clouds.

- Notice the sounds in the room; just notice, don't judge. Just be.

- From your perspective of looking at a vast, open sky, notice the sounds, your thoughts, your feelings. Just notice. See them passing…

- Throughout, notice the rhythm of your breathing. Taking place all by itself. The Holy Spirit, the Breath of Life.

- Visualize Him pouring oil onto the top of your head… follow the flow – running down your neck, over your shoulders and chest, pooling in your breathing centre, and letting some run down your knees, your shins, and onto your feet.

- Tell Him that He is your centre; He is your Breath of Life.

- When you are ready…

- Wriggle your toes, move your feet, shake your shoulders…

- Stretch and end the exercise.

Appendix 2

Recommended websites and books

www.alzheimers.org.uk

www.dementiauk.org

www.gloriousopportunity.org

www.nhs.uk

www.pilgrimsfriend.org.uk

Jill Bolte Taylor, *My Stroke of Insight*, Hodder Paperbacks, 2009

Dennis Greenberger and Christine Padesky, *Mind Over Mood: Change How You Feel By Changing the Way You Think*, Guilford Press, 1995

Tom Kitwood, *Dementia Reconsidered*, Oxford University Press, 2009

Caroline Leaf, *Who Switched off My Brain: Controlling Toxic Thoughts and Emotions*, Thomas Nelson, 2009

Louise Morse, *Dementia: Frank and Linda's Story, New Understanding, New Approaches, New Hope*, Monarch Books, 2010

Louise Morse, *Could It Be Dementia? Losing Your Mind Doesn't Mean Losing Your Soul*, Monarch Books, 2008

Louise Morse, *Worshipping with Dementia*, Monarch Books, 2010

Dr Max Pemberton, *Stop Smoking with CBT*, Ebury Digital, 2015

Andrew White, *Faith under Fire*, Monarch Books, 2013

Graham Stokes, *And Still the Music Plays: Stories of People with Dementia*, Hawker Publications Ltd, 2010

Graham Stokes, *Challenging Behaviour in Dementia: A Person-Centred Approach*, Speechmark, 2014

Norman H Wright, *Making Peace with Your Past*, Revell, 1987

People with dementia and their caregivers often feel very much alone and deserted. They feel that people avoid them, and that they are misunderstood. They experience a tumult of hurtful emotions. It helps to read those expressed by the writers of the psalms.

> *Be merciful to me, Lord, for I am in distress;*
> *my eyes grow weak with sorrow,*
> *my soul and body with grief.*
> *My life is consumed by anguish*
> *and my years by groaning;*
> *my strength fails because of my affliction,*
> *and my bones grow weak...*
> *I am the utter contempt of my neighbours*
> *and an object of dread to my closest friends –*
> *those who see me on the street flee from me.*
> *I am forgotten as though I were dead;*
> *I have become like broken pottery.*
> *For I hear many whispering,*
> *"Terror on every side!"*
> *They conspire against me and plot to take my life.*
> *(Psalm 31:9–13)*

> *All my longings lie open before you, Lord;*
> *my sighing is not hidden from you.*
> *My heart pounds, my strength fails me;*
> *even the light has gone from my eyes.*
> *My friends and companions avoid me because of my wounds;*
> *my neighbours stay far away.*
> *(Psalm 38:9–11)*

All my enemies whisper together against me;
they imagine the worst for me, saying,
"A vile disease has afflicted him;
he will never get up from the place where he lies."
Even my close friend,
someone I trusted,
one who shared my bread,
has turned against me.
(Psalm 41:7–9)

God never leaves us

Who shall separate us from the love of Christ? Shall
trouble or hardship or persecution or famine or
nakedness or danger or sword? (Romans 8:35)

Don't you know that you yourselves are God's temple
and that God's Spirit lives in you? (1 Corinthians 3:16)

Yet I am always with you;
You hold me by my right hand.
You guide me with Your counsel,
and afterward You will take me into glory.
Whom have I in heaven but you?
And earth has nothing I desire besides You.
My flesh and my heart may fail,
but God is the strength of my heart and my portion
forever. (Psalm 73:23–26)

Do not fear, for I have redeemed you;
I have summoned you by name; you are mine.
When you pass through the waters,

I will be with you;
and when you pass through the rivers,
they will not sweep over you.
When you walk through the fire,
you will not be burned;
the flames will not set you ablaze.
For I am the Lord your God,
the Holy One of Israel, your Saviour;
I give Egypt for your ransom,
Cush and Seba in your stead.
(Isaiah 43:1–3)

I give them eternal life, and they shall never perish; no one will snatch them out of my hand. My Father, who has given them to me, is greater than all; no one can snatch them out of my Father's hand. I and the Father are one. (John 10:28–30)

A bruised reed he will not break,
and a smouldering wick He will not snuff out,
till He has brought justice through to victory.
(Matthew 12:20)

And we know that in all things God works for the good of those who love Him, who have been called according to his purpose. For those God foreknew he also predestined to be conformed to the image of his Son, that he might be the firstborn among many brothers and sisters. And those He predestined, He also called; those He called, He also justified; those He justified, He also glorified. (Romans 8:28–31)

Nevertheless, God's solid foundation stands firm,
sealed with this inscription: "The Lord knows those
who are his ..." (2 Timothy 2:19)

The Holy Spirit gives support and encouragement

"Never will I leave you;
never will I forsake you."
So we say with confidence,
"The Lord is my helper;
I will not be afraid.
What can mere mortals do to me?
(Hebrews 13:5–6)

As a father has compassion on his children,
so the Lord has compassion on those who fear Him;
for he knows how we are formed,
he remembers that we are dust.
(Psalm 103:13–14)

For by You I can run upon a troop; by my God I can
leap over a wall. (2 Samuel 22:30, NASB)

Then Jesus said to his disciples: "Therefore I tell you,
do not worry about your life, what you will eat; or
about your body, what you will wear. For life is more
than food, and the body more than clothes. Consider
the ravens: They do not sow or reap, they have no
storeroom or barn; yet God feeds them. And how much
more valuable you are than birds! Who of you by
worrying can add a single hour to your life?
(Luke 12:22–25)

Though I walk in the midst of trouble,
You will revive me;
You will stretch forth Your hand against the wrath of
my enemies,
and Your right hand will save me.
The Lord will accomplish what concerns me;
Your loving kindness, O Lord, is everlasting;
do not forsake the works of Your hands.
(Psalm 138:7–8, NASB)

I can do all things through Christ who strengthens me.
(Philippians 4:13, NKJV)

And God is able to make all grace abound to you, so that
in all things at all times, having all that you need, you
will abound in every good work. (2 Corinthians 9:8)

No eye has seen, no ear has heard, no mind has
conceived what God has prepared for those who love
Him. (1 Corinthians 2:9)

Trust in the Lord with all your heart, and do not
lean on your own understanding. In all your ways
acknowledge Him, and He will make your paths
straight. (Proverbs 3:5–6, ESV)

Taking care of yourself

Watch over your heart with all diligence, for from it
flow the springs of life. (Proverbs 4:23, NASB)

For as he thinketh in his heart, so is he.
(Proverbs 23:7, KJV)

Be renewed in the spirit of your mind.
(Ephesians 4:23, KJV)

We take captive every thought to make it obedient to Christ. (2 Corinthians 10:5)

Which of you by worrying can add one cubit to his stature?… Therefore, do not worry about tomorrow, for tomorrow will worry about its own things. Sufficient for the day is its own trouble. (Matthew 6:27, 34, NKJV)

Casting all your care upon Him, for He cares for you. (1 Peter 5:7, NKJV)

Blessed are those who mourn, for they shall be comforted. (Matthew 5:4, NKJV)

And the peace of God, which transcends all understanding, will guard your hearts and your minds in Christ Jesus. (Philippians 4:7)

Come to Me, all you who labour and are heavy laden, and I will give you rest. (Matthew 11:28, NKJV)

Finally

May our Lord Jesus Christ himself and God our Father, who loved us and by His grace gave us eternal encouragement and good hope, encourage your hearts and strengthen you in every good deed and word. (2 Thessalonians 2:16-17)